WHAT?

ERIN McHUGH

Sterling Publishing Co., Inc.
New York

Library of Congress Cataloging-in-Publication Data Available

10   9   8   7   6   5   4   3   2   1

Published by Sterling Publishing Co., Inc.
387 Park Avenue South, New York, NY 10016
© 2005 by Erin McHugh
Distributed in Canada by Sterling Publishing
^c/o Canadian Manda Group, 165 Dufferin Street
Toronto, Ontario, Canada M6K 3H6
Distributed in Great Britain by Chrysalis Books Group PLC
The Chrysalis Building, Bramley Road, London W10 6SP, England
Distributed in Australia by Capricorn Link (Australia) Pty. Ltd.
P.O. Box 704, Windsor, NSW 2756, Australia

Manufactured in the United States of America
All rights reserved

Sterling ISBN 1-4027-2570-1

For information about custom editions, special sales, premium and
corporate purchases, please contact Sterling Special Sales
Department at 800-805-5489 or specialsales@sterlingpub.com.

WHAT?

OSCAR AND THE OSCARINIS

In 1938, Walt Disney won an Academy Award for his animated feature *Snow White and the Seven Dwarfs*—or, more precisely, he received one for himself, and seven miniatures for his little friends.

◆

MANILA FOLDERS are made from and named after Manila hemp, or abaca, a sturdy fiber derived from a relative of the banana plant. Indigenous to the Philippines, its light weight, durability, and strength make it a natural choice for paper products.

◆

POLITICAL PARTY

The signers of the United States Constitution apparently had a "work hard, play hard" mentality. Just two days before signing, they ordered a few drinks. When the bill came, it included:

> 54 bottles of Madeira
> 60 bottles of claret
> 30 to 50 bottles of whiskey, beer, hard cider, and port
> 7 bowls of spiked punch

◆

Many experts believe that the back brace PRESIDENT KENNEDY wore on November 22, 1963, was part of the reason he didn't survive the assassination in Dallas. The first bullet passed through his neck, but did not kill him. However, Kennedy's back brace prevented his body from slumping over, leaving a clear target for the second bullet, a fatal shot to his head.

COP TALK

"10-4, over and out!" is just one code in the lexicon of police jargon, some of which we've learned from watching television cop shows. Although the codes vary between police departments, here are some examples:

10-1	You are being received poorly
10-10	Fight in progress
10-15	Civil disturbance
10-16	Pick up prisoners
10-24	Trouble at station
10-31	Crime in progress
10-32	Person with gun
10-34	Riot
10-39	Urgent—use light and siren
10-45	Animal carcass
10-79	Notify coroner
10-80	Vacation check
10-85	Will be late
10-90	Bank alarm
10-94	Drag race
10-98	Jailbreak
11-12	Dead animal/loose livestock
11-14	Animal bite
11-15	Ball game in street
code 7	Out for lunch
187	Homicide
288	Lewd conduct
311	Indecent exposure
390D	Drunk unconscious
415G	Gang disturbance
470	Forgery

595	Runaway car
903L	Low-flying aircraft
905V	Vicious animal
908	Begging
914H	Heart attack
915	Dumping rubbish
921P	Peeping Tom
927	Suspicious person
927A	Person pulled from telephone
949	Gasoline spill
962	Suspect is armed and dangerous
975	Can your suspect hear your radio?
967	Outlaw motorcyclists
966	Sniper
995	Labor trouble
996	Explosive
5150	Mental case
21958	Drunk pedestrian in roadway

◆

STERLING SERVICE
The Proper Setting for the Elegant Table

Left of the Plate	*Above the Plate*
Napkin	Butter knife (on butter plate)
Fish fork	Dessert spoon (bowl left)
Dinner fork	Cake fork (tines right)
Salad fork	
	Crystal or glassware
Right of Plate	*(from left to right)*
Service knife	Water glass
Fish knife	Red wineglass
Soup spoon	White wineglass

MAD FADS
Nutty Obsessions of the Twentieth Century

1920s

Flagpole sitting
Flappers
Freudianism
Mah Jongg
Dance marathons

1930s

Stamp collecting
Board games
Drive-in movies
Miniature golf
Zoot suits

1940s

Swallowing goldfish
Silly putty
Pea shooters
"Kilroy was here"
Slinky

1950s

Phone booth stuffing
Hula hoop
3-D movies
Coonskin caps
Panty raids

1960s

The Twist
Fallout shelters
Troll dolls
Ouija boards
Bouffants

1970s

String art
Streaking
Puka shells
Mexican jumping beans
Pet rocks

1980s

Rubik's Cube
Boom boxes
Cabbage Patch dolls
Break dancing
Smurfs

1990s

Beanie Babies
Grunge
Furby
Tattoos
Piercing

WHO—AND WHAT—AM I?

Autosomal DNA determines much of who we are, and consists of all of a cell's DNA, except the X and Y chromosomes and the mitochondrial DNA. Fifty percent of your autosomal DNA comes from your father, and 50 percent comes from your mother, and it contains a broad picture of your genetic ancestry. It is currently used to legally verify Native American blood when questions of land inheritance arise.

THE FEATHER LAW

Federal laws that prohibit the killing, possession, or use of several types of birds, such as the bald eagle, were enacted to protect various bird species from hunters, but Native Americans enrolled in federally recognized tribes may legally possess eagle feathers for use in religious ceremonies. A provision mandates that these feathers be obtained, via permit, from a central distribution office and they cannot be sold, bartered, or given away to anyone other than another enrolled member of a federally recognized tribe.

◆

SOCIAL SECURITY currently offers U.S. citizens four types of protection:

1. Retirement benefits
2. Survivors' benefits
3. Disability benefits
4. Medicare medical insurance benefits

◆

Ancient Romans considered FLAMINGO TONGUES a delicacy.

THE PULITZER PRIZE

All winners, except for Public Service, are awarded a $10,000 cash prize and a certificate of recognition. The Public Service Award winner receives a gold medal.

Current Pulitzer Prize Categories

Beat Reporting
Biography or Autobiography
Breaking News Photography
Breaking News Reporting
Commentary
Criticism
Drama
Editorial Cartooning
Editorial Writing
Explanatory Reporting
Feature Photography
Feature Writing
Fiction
General Non-Fiction
History
International Reporting
Investigative Reporting
Music
National Reporting
Public Service
Biography or Autobiography (by an American author)
Fiction (by an American author)
General Non-Fiction (by an American author)
U.S. History
Poetry

Discontinued Pulitzer Prize Categories

Correspondence
Explanatory Journalism (replaced by Explanatory Reporting)
General News Reporting
Local General or Spot News Reporting
Local Investigative Specialized Reporting
Local Reporting
Local Reporting, Edition Time
Local Reporting, No Edition Time
The Novel (now the Pulitzer Prize for Fiction)
Photography (replaced by Feature Photography
    and Breaking News Photography)
Specialized Reporting
Spot News Photography
Spot News Reporting
Telegraphic Reporting—National and Internationa

◆

THE EMANCIPATION PROCLAMATION

When it was enacted on New Year's Day 1863, Abraham
Lincoln called the Emancipation Proclamation "a fit and
necessary war measure for suppressing rebellion." Lincoln's
proclamation applied only to freed slaves in Southern states
that had already seceded from the Union, making it virtually
unenforceable. It did not apply to slaves in the North, nor in
the border states of Delaware, Maryland, Kentucky, and
Missouri. It was not until 1865, when Congress passed the
Thirteenth Amendment, that slavery was abolished in the
United States.

◆

PEARLS will dissolve in vinegar.

THE NOBEL PRIZE

Since their first presentation in 1901, Nobel laureates have received a cash prize, a gold medal, and a diploma. Winners can be either individuals or institutions and currently share approximately US$1.3 million per category. There can be up to three winners per category, with all winners for each category dividing the prize money. A prize may not be awarded if no candidate is chosen, but each prize must be awarded at least once every five years. Any money declined by laureates remains the property of the Nobel Prize Foundation and remains in its trust.

Nobel Prize categories

Nobel Prize in Chemistry
Nobel Prize in Economic Sciences*
Nobel Prize in Literature
Nobel Prize in Physics
Nobel Prize in Physiology or Medicine
Nobel Peace Prize

*Instituted in 1968 by the Bank of Sweden in Memory of Alfred Nobel, founder of the Nobel Prize.

◆

The JOLLY ROGER is an English euphemism for a pirate flag and is thought by some to come from the French "joli rouge" or "pretty red," a wry description of the red banner flown by pirates that declared they would show no mercy to victims. Seventeenth-century privateers designed their own personal banners, often flown along with the national flag, and what we think of today as the Jolly Roger—the skull and crossbones on a black background—first appeared on the high seas in the eighteenth century. It may have come from the captain's log, in which the skull and crossbones indicated the death of a crew member.

"I SAY, OLD CHAP"

For the feel of Hollywood in its heyday or an afternoon at the races, when it comes to men's neckwear, only an ascot will do. Here is how it's properly tied:

1. Pull the ascot around the back of your neck as you would a tie. Let the left end hang slightly more than two inches longer than the right.
2. Wrap the left end one and a half times over the right. Continue around as if you were going to complete a second turn, and push the left end up through the neck loop so that it emerges over the top.
3. Center the top flap so that it is the only visible portion of the ascot. Spread the sides slightly, creating a "waterfall" of fabric from the base of your neck.
4. Undo only one button of your shirt. Tuck the ends of the ascot into your shirt.
5. Secure the ends of the ascot with a stick pin if desired.

◆

AMERICA'S CUP?

The America's Cup, often called the oldest trophy in sports, did not travel from its home in the New York Yacht Club from 1851 until 1983, when it was won by an Australian team. The cup has since resided in San Diego; Sydney, Australia; and Auckland, New Zealand; and has taken a trip back to its original home, the Royal Yacht Squadron in Cowes, England. The cup always flies accompanied by two security guards in its own seat in business class. It also has its own specially crafted Louis Vuitton travel case, so that it may travel in comfort and style.

SPEED RACKING

In bars, the good liquor, referred to as "top shelf," is kept behind the bartender, and the least expensive liquor, called "well drinks," is kept in what is called the "speed rack," below the lip of the bar. They usually line up, left to right, in the following order: vodka, bourbon, gin, scotch, rum, brandy, tequila, triple sec, rye, and kahlua.

◆

WHAT DID YOU SAY?

The longest word (containing forty-five letters) currently listed in any dictionary is pneumonoultramicroscopicsilicovol-canoconiosis and is defined in *Webster's Third New International Dictionary, Unabridged* as "a pneumoconiosis caused by the inhalation of very fine silicate or quartz dust and occurring especially in miners." This easily beats the more familiar antidisestablishmentarianism (the only one of the über-long words that is not science-based), which has a mere twenty-eight letters. Other contenders are:

Otorhinolaryngological	22 letters
Immunoelectrophoretically	25 letters
Psychophysicotherapeutics	25 letters
Thyroparathyroidectomized	25 letters
Pneumoencephalographically	26 letters
Radioimmunoelectrophoresis	26 letters
Psychoneuroendocrinological	27 letters
Hepaticocholangiogastrostomy	28 letters
Spectrophotofluorometrically	28 letters
Pseudopseudohypoparathyroidism	30 letter

MUSICAL JEWELS

In 1958 the Recording Industry Association of America began issuing award records—a facsimile disc mounted on a plaque—as industry recognition of top-selling recordings based on their audits. Originally a gold record was presented in recognition of 500,000 copies sold. Along with the explosive growth and rapid technological changes of recent decades came recording industry changes. RIAA announced different award levels, adding the Platinum record in 1976 and Multi-Platinum in 1984, and introduced a diamond record award in 1999. Currently the awards are based on U.S. unit sales (including military post exchanges abroad) and are:

Record	Number Sold
Gold	500,000
Platinum	1,000,000
Multi-Platinum	2,000,000
Diamond	10,000,000

The number sold to receive one of these awards is the same, whether the record is a single or an album.

DR. BUNTING TO THE RESCUE

Noxzema is a trademark name with a personal history. Soon after its invention, it was marketed as an efficient cold cream as well as a remedy for relieving sunburn under the name "Dr. Bunting's Sunburn Remedy." Shortly after its introduction, a surprised and happy customer wrote to the company, reporting, "Your cream knocked my eczema!" and a new name and use were announced for the remedy.

WHAT ARE THE 6,469,952 BLACK SPOTS ON THAT SCREEN?

They are the total number of spots that appear on the dogs in the animated film *101 Dalmatians*.

◆

SOMNAMBULISM

If you're worried that you walk in your sleep and have a vague memory of doing so, you may be right: About 18 percent of the population does so at least once during their lifetime. The majority of somnambulists are prepubescent, and their somnambulism is unlikely to last through their teens. However, if childhood sleepwalking begins after the age of nine, it will often last well into adulthood.

Autonomic (independently functioning) behavior during somnambulism can involve dressing, eating, and, rarely, criminal or harmful activity. Here are a few helpful hints should you suddenly discover you're strolling during the night:

- Being overtired can trigger a sleepwalking episode; be sure to get enough rest.
- Practice meditation or perform relaxation exercises to calm yourself before going to sleep.
- Remove anything from the bedroom that could be dangerous to you when sleepwalking.
- Sleep on the ground floor if possible.
- Carefully review with your physician any current medications you're taking.
- Try a hypnotherapy treatment.

SOME KIND OF HOT

The substance in chili peppers that makes them hot is called capsaicin. In 1912, pharmacist Wilbur Scoville created a scale to measure pepper hotness using a solution of pepper extract that was diluted in increasing amounts of sugar water until the "heat" of the pepper was no longer detectable to a panel of (usually five) tasters. Scoville developed Scoville Units as a measure, with 0 being no heat and with heat increasing along with the Scoville Unit number. Pure capsaicin would measure 16 million Scoville Units.

Type of Pepper	*Number of Scoville Units*
Habanero	100,000–350,000
Tien tsin	40,000–60,000
Dundicut	40,000–60,000
Cayenne	30,000–50,000
de Arbol	15,000–30,000
Ground hot red	20,000
Serrano	5,000–15,000
Chipotle pepper	5,000–10,000
Jalapeño	2,500–8,000
Ancho pepper	1,000–3,000

◆

451° FAHRENHEIT is the temperature at which paper will ignite and books will burn, according to Ray Bradbury's horrific tale of the future, *Fahrenheit 451*. The novel, and the movie adapted from it, takes place in what is known as a dystopia, a fictional society that is the opposite of utopia, usually existing in the future, when conditions of life are extremely bad, often due to deprivation, oppression, or terror.

PORTMANTEAUS
A Short List of "Blended" Words—New Words
Formed by Joining Two Words

Anacronym	From anachronism and acronym
Backronym	From back and acronym
Blaxploitation	From black and exploitation
Bootylicious	From booty and delicious (as sung by Destiny's Child)
Chortle	From chuckle and snort (coined by Lewis Carroll)
Cocacolonization	From Coca-Cola and colonization
Corpsicle	From corpse and Popsicle
Cyborg	From cybernetic and organism
Digipeater	From digital and repeater
Dramedy	From drama and comedy
Ebonics	From ebony and phonics
Ecoteur	From ecological and saboteur
Ginormous	From gigantic and enormous
Guesstimate	From guess and estimate
Hasbian	From has been and lesbian
Jazzercise	From jazz and exercise
Mantastic	From man and fantastic
Mockumentary	From mock and documentary
Moped	From motor and pedal
Motel	From motor and hotel
Oxbridge	From Oxford and Cambridge
Posistor	From positive and thermistor
Procrasturbate	From procrastinate and masturbate
Sexcellent	From sex and excellent
Sexercise	From sex and exercise
Skort	From skirt and short (as in short pants)
Smog	From smoke and fog

Soundscape	From sound and landscape
Spork	From spoon and fork
Squiggle	From squirm and wiggle
Stagflation	From stagnation and inflation
Swaption	From swap and option
Tangelo	From tangerine and pomelo
Televangelist	From television and evangelist
Woon	From wooden and spoon (flat wooden utensils for eating dished ice cream)

OH, REINDEER!

They may be caribou to you:

1. They are approximately three and a half feet in height.
2. They run about fifty miles per hour at top speed.
3. They weigh more than three hundred pounds, and can carry up to their own weight.
4. Both males and females have antlers.
5. Their milk is used for drinking and making cheese in Lapland.
6. They live in Europe, Asia, Alaska, and Canada.
7. Their skins are used to make clothing and tents.
8. They *are* used to pull sleighs.

NINE-BANDED ARMADILLOS (the variety found in the U.S.) are always born as same-sex identical quadruplets. They will often eat forty thousand ants in a single sitting and are excellent in water, able to hold their breath for up to ten minutes by inhaling air into their lungs, stomach, and intestines (which can also make them buoyant). Letting their breath out enables armadillos to feed by walking along the bottom of a body of water.

SWORN STATEMENT

The presidential oath of office is taken by every president of the United States on first entering office, as specified in Article II, Section 1 of the Constitution:

I do solemnly swear (or affirm) that I will faithfully execute the office of President of the United States, and will to the best of my ability, preserve, protect, and defend the Constitution of the United States.

The "affirm" option is given the president-elect because members of the Quaker religion do not swear on a Bible (this is also true for any Quaker serving as a witness in court).

A FEW FACTS ABOUT THE FAIR FOWL
All Things Chicken

Bantam or banty: A small version of a large fowl
Pullet: Young female chicken who has not yet begun to lay eggs
Capon: A castrated rooster
Chanticleer: A loud crower
Cock or rooster: Adult male of the domestic fowl
Cockerel: A young, male, domesticated fowl
Hen: A mature female of the common domestic fowl
Bantamweight: 118 pounds and under (usually refers to a human)

A cock has no penis. He and the hen both have a single orifice called a *cloaca* (from the Latin word for sewer), which serves a multitude of functions, including reproduction.

NO-WAY BAY

Items that can't be sold on eBay include:

alcohol * animals and wildlife products * cable TV
descramblers * counterfeit items * current catalogs *
drugs and drug paraphernalia * embargoed goods * firearms *
fireworks * government IDs and licenses * human body parts *
lock-picking devices * lottery tickets * postage meters *
prescription drugs and materials * recalled items * stocks
and other securities * stolen property * surveillance
equipment * tobacco

WHAT IS BEYOND BEYOND?

There is a number so incomprehensible it is rarely used, even
in physics and astronomy. In 1938, mathematician Edward
Kasner asked his nine-year-old nephew, Milton Sirotta, to
come up with a name for the number that Kasner had
invented, a one followed by 100 zeroes. "Googol" was little
Milton's big idea, and if that's not big enough, there's
googolplex, which is defined as one to the power of googol.
A googolplex is written like this:

$$10^{10^{100}}$$

The largest number ever in a real mathematical problem is
called Graham's Number, for Ronald L. Graham, a juggler,
acrobat, and mathematician. It is incomprehensibly large, and
occurs in combinatorics, the branch of mathematics that
studies the enumeration, combination, and permutation of
sets of elements and the mathematical relations that char-
acterize their properties. It is often used in probability and
statistics.

SOME JACKPOT!

The largest individual lottery win came to an incredible $314.9 million and was won by Andrew "Jack" Whittaker Jr. of Scott Depot, West Virginia, in 2002. He took half the prize in a lump sum of $111.7 million after taxes rather than the full prize in thirty annual installments. Whittaker tithed a tenth of his winnings to his church and created a foundation for the less-fortunate citizens of West Virginia, which he has subsequently closed. Alas, he lost some of his winnings while at a West Virginia nightclub, where he was robbed of a suitcase containing $545,000 in cash and cashiers' checks. He has also been arrested for drunk driving twice, has been in rehab, and has been involved in a number of lawsuits. You win some, you lose some.

◆

No WORD in the English language rhymes with:

month * nothing * orange * pint * purple * silver

◆

SNAKE-EATING SNAKES

What kind of snake would pick on another snake? The larger of the two, naturally, normally preys on the smaller snake; it's nature's way.

Asian coral snake	Krait
Black-headed python	North American king snake
Burrowing asp	Ring-necked snake
King snake	Texas coral snake
King cobra	

ADDING COMPLICATIONS

The annual Rube Goldberg Machine Contest celebrates the Pulitzer Prize winner's "Invention" cartoons. Entrants eschew conventional problem solving, relying instead on imagination and intuition to create the most convoluted solutions possible. Goldberg (1883–1970) said his inventions—or, more precisely, noninventions—were symbolic of man's capacity for exerting maximum effort to accomplish minimal results. He believed there were two ways to do things: the simple way and the hard way, and many people prefer the hard way. The 2005 challenge asked entrants to remove the old batteries from a two-battery flashlight, install new batteries, and turn the flashlight on—in twenty or more steps. Other recent twenty steps–plus challenges have been:

1988	Adhere a stamp to a letter
1989	Sharpen a pencil
1990	Put the lid on a ball jar
1991	Toast a slice of bread
1992	Unlock a combination padlock
1993	Screw a lightbulb into a socket
1994	Make a cup of coffee
1995	Turn on a radio
1996	Put coins in a bank
1997	Insert and then play a CD
1998	Shut off an alarm clock
1999	Set a golf tee and tee up a golf ball
2000	Fill, seal a time capsule with 20th-century inventions
2001	Select, clean, and peel an apple
2002	Select, raise, and wave a national flag
2003	Select, crush, and recycle an empty soft-drink can
2004	Select, mark, and cast an election ballot

HALLS OF FAME

They're not just for ballplayers anymore. Here are some
lesser-known halls of fame that honor the best of their best:

Accounting	Great Americans
Advertising	Hamburgers
Afro-Americans	Hollywood Stuntmen
Agriculture	Hot Dogs
Astronauts	Inventors
Automotive	Jewish-Americans
Aviation	Nashville Songwriters
Business	National Teachers
Burlesque	National Women
Car Collectors	Nurses
Checkers	Photography
Chess	Police
Circus	Quilters
Classical Music	Rivers
Clowns	Rock and Roll
Comedy	RVs/Motor Homes
Country Music	Songwriters
Cowgirls	Space
Ecology	

IT'S FLOTSAM OR JETSAM

Both words originally pertained to the sea: *Flotsam* in mari-
time law applies to wreckage or cargo left floating on the sea
after a shipwreck. *Jetsam* applies to cargo or equipment
thrown overboard (jettisoned) from a ship in distress and
either sunk or washed ashore. The common phrase *flotsam
and jetsam* is now used loosely to describe any objects found
floating or washed ashore.

DID I DREAM THAT?

Sea monkeys are indeed real; here are a few facts:

- Sea monkeys are actually a type of brine shrimp, *Artemia salina*.
- Sea monkeys breathe through their feet.
- Sea monkey eggs can survive for years without water by hibernating.
- Sea monkeys are born with one eye but develop two more.
- Sea monkeys are attracted to light and can be taught tricks with a flashlight.
- Sea monkeys require water and feeding only every five days.
- If sea monkeys are not bred on their own in captivity, they will be eaten by other inhabitants of the deep (or not-so-deep: never put them in a tank with other fish).

WORDS OF WISDOM

According to the 1893 *Farmer's Almanac* (the first edition of that now-ubiquitous book) the four things that should never flatter us are:

1. Familiarity with the great
2. The caresses of women
3. The smiles of our enemies
4. A warm day in winter

The word UMLAUT doesn't have one. (It's the double dot over the "u.")

STEP RIGHT UP, LADIES AND FLEAS!

Although already centuries old, the flea circus became the talk of London during the 1830s, due to L. Bertolotto, the P. T. Barnum of his time. Bertolotto had flea orchestras playing audible flea music, flea foursomes in games of flea whist, and flea waltzing, complete with dresses and frock coats. Fleas drew miniature coaches, carried guns, and fired cannons "not larger than a common pin," and fleas dressed as Napoleon and the Duke of Wellington. Bertolotto's flea circus became so popular that other impresarios developed their own flea extravaganzas, with flea circuses becoming popular fixtures in carnivals and circus sideshows throughout Europe and the United States. As late as the 1950s there was a popular flea circus near New York's Times Square. A lot has been written about the "condition" of the fleas—dead or alive—and many flea circus acts relied on dead fleas glued to their seats, to tightropes, or to other circus equipment, or on fleas manipulated by magnets hidden below a tiny flea stage. Bertolotto's playbill announced that his superior flea equipment "precludes all charges of cruelty to the fleas." Other acts, also refuting such tricks, had fleas rigged in wire harnesses so the fleas could move in only a particular manner.

Today flea circus ringmasters control their "trained" performers using several odd and sometimes difficult methods. A trainer can limit the height of a flea's jump, for example, with a glass ceiling, or by having the flea in a test tube lying on its side. (Fleas don't like to bump their heads.) And certain chemicals will bother a flea: Put some on a small ball and fleas will push it away with their legs, giving the illusion that they are playing football. Their sensitivity to heat and light can also be used to manipulate appearances—or perform tricks, if you will—by forcing them to move in a specific direction. Following, some little-known flea facts:

- There is said to be a flea in a Kiev museum that wears horseshoes made of real gold.
- A flea may be able to pull up to 160,000 times its own weight.
- A flea can jump over 200 times its own height.
- When jumping, the flea accelerates faster than the space shuttle.
- Fleas can jump 30,000 times without a break.
- It was popular in the 1920s to collect dead fleas dressed as wedding couples.
- Fleas are attracted to carbon dioxide.

WINNING WORDS AT THE NATIONAL SPELLING BEE

Spelling bees are almost always won or lost because of one word. Here are some winners:

Easy	*More Difficult*
Fracas	Schappe
Deteriorating	Syllepsis
Knack	Troche
Therapy	Cacolet
Interning	Hydrophyte
Sanatarium	Elucubrate
Initials	Odontalgia
Luge	Elegiacal
Deification	Spoliator
Incisor	Fibranne
Abalone	Antipyretic
Chihuahua	Xanthosis
Croissant	Euonym
Sycophant	Succedaneum

IT OUGHTA BE ILLEGAL

And apparently—at least in some places—it is. A few oddities that are against the law:

Have sexual relations with a porcupine in Florida

Pay a debt higher than 25 cents with pennies in Canada

Fall asleep under a hair dryer in Florida, even if you're the salon owner

Kill or even threaten a butterfly in Pacific Grove, California

Duel in Paraguay if both parties are not registered blood donors

Have sex in a butcher shop's meat freezer in Newcastle, Wyoming

Hunt camels in the state of Arizona

Have sex on a parked motorcycle in London, England

Wear a fake mustache that causes laughter in church in Alabama

Bar owners in Nebraska may not sell beer unless they have a kettle of soup on the stove

Beer and pretzels cannot be served at the same time in any bar or restaurant in North Dakota

Throw a ball at someone's head for fun in New York

Lie down and fall asleep with your shoes on in North Dakota

Get a fish drunk in Ohio

Tie a giraffe to a telephone pole or street lamp in Atlanta, Georgia

"POWDER OF SYMPATHY"

One longitudinal theory proposed in 1688 employed a substance made primarily of sulfuric acid and was called the "Powder of Sympathy."

It was believed that a person who had been stabbed, no matter how long ago, would feel the same intensity of pain when Powder of Sympathy was sprinkled onto the same knife that caused the original wound. It became a popular medical treatment in the seventeenth century, and patients often jumped or swooned when practitioners powdered swords that had cut them or cloths that had dressed their wounds.

During that century it was believed that if dogs, all wounded by the same knife, were placed on each of His Majesty's ships and every day at Greenwich time noon that same knife was plunged into a bowl full of the Powder of Sympathy, all the dogs on every ship would yelp, no matter where they were. Ship captains would then know that it was exactly noon in Greenwich, England, and could calculate their longitude from this.

◆

The SWEDES invented a kind of ladies' glove that was made of leather and worked to have a slight nap on one side by brushing the smooth surface with an emery board. The French gave it a name—suede—which is French for "Swedish." Today suede is buffed and brushed in essentially the same manner.

◆

The PETER PRINCIPLE decrees: "In a hierarchy, every employee tends to rise to his level of incompetence."

THE LAST WORD ON DADAISM

Dada, or *Dadaism* (French, from *dada,* a child's word for horse) was a Nihilistic art movement that flourished chiefly in France, Switzerland, and Germany from about 1916 to 1920, and was based on the principles of deliberate irrationality, anarchy, and cynicism, and which rejected laws of beauty and social organization.

Views on Dada from the Artists Themselves

Dada is beautiful like the night, who cradles the
young day in her arms.
—Hans Arp

Dada speaks with you, it is everything,
it envelops everything, it belongs to every religion, can be
neither victory nor defeat, it lives in space and not in time.
—Francis Picabia

Dada is the sun, Dada is the egg. Dada is the
Police of the Police.
—Ricard Huelsenbeck

Dada doubts everything. Dada is an armadillo.
Everything is Dada, too. Beware of Dada. Anti-dadaism is
a disease: self-kleptomania, man's normal condition, is Dada.
But the real Dadas are against Dada.
—Tristan Tzara

MEET THE PRESS debuted on NBC in 1947 and continues to hold the record as television's longest-running program. It was also TV's first news show.

USEFUL YIDDISH PUTDOWNS

shikker	drunkard
shkapeh	hag
shlak	a nuisance
shlatten shammes	busybody
shlecht veib	shrew
shlemiel	dope, fool
shlimazel	unlucky person
shlooche	slut
shlub	stupid person
shlump	sloppy person
shmendrick	nincompoop
shmoe	dunce
shmuck	self-made fool
shnook	patsy
shnorrer	beggar
shtunk	lousy human being

◆

TEN STEPS TO A DECATHLON MEDAL
The Events That Comprise the Two-Day Olympic Decathlon

Day 1	*Day 2*
100-meter run	110-meter hurdles
Long jump	Discus throw
Shot put	Pole vault
High jump	Javelin throw
400-meter run	1,500-meter run

WHAT WAS SERVED AT THE LAST SUPPER?

Many believe the Last Supper was actually a seder. Jesus and the apostles were served:

- Passover lamb to remind them of the lambs' blood sprinkled on their doors so that the Angel of Death would spare the firstborn of the Jews
- Unleavened bread to remind them of the haste with which their ancestors left Egypt
- Salt water to remind them of the many tears shed during the years of slavery in Egypt
- Bitter herbs to remind them of the bitterness of slavery
- A sweet mixture of apples, dates, pomegranate, nuts, and cinnamon sticks, to symbolize the clay and straw their ancestors used to make bricks while in slavery
- Four cups of wine during the course of the meal to remind them of the four promises of God's deliverance in Exodus 6:6–7

◆

CATS ENTERTAINMENT!

The top ten longest-running Broadway plays of all time:

1. Cats
2. The Phantom of the Opera
3. Les Misérables
4. A Chorus Line
5. Oh! Calcutta!
6. Beauty and the Beast
7. Miss Saigon
8. Rent
9. 42nd Street
10. Grease

CONTINENTAL DIVIDES

The basic definition of a continent requires that it be a large, nonsubmerged land mass, and that it have geologically significant borders. As the definition is so vague, some sources list as few as four or five continents, although it is commonly acknowledged that there are six—the generally accepted geologists' count—or seven:

Seven continents: Africa, Antarctica, Asia, Europe, North America, Oceania, South America

Six continents: Africa, Antarctica, Oceania, Eurasia, North America, and South America

Six continents: Africa, America, Antarctica, Asia, Oceania, and Europe

Five continents: Africa, America, Oceania, Antarctica, Eurasia

Five continents: Africa, America, Oceania, Europe, Asia

Four continents: America, Oceania, Antarctica, Eurafrasia

Various Continental Definitions

Eurasia: Europe and Asia

Eurafrasia: Europe, Africa, and Asia

Oceania: A name used for varying groups of islands of the Pacific Ocean. In its narrow usage it refers to Polynesia (including New Zealand), Melanesia (including New Guinea), and Micronesia. In its wider usage it includes Australia.

RELATIVE RELATIONSHIPS

Relationships are hard enough—understanding the complex terms of genealogy is even more confusing:

Cousin is the term used to signify the relationship between the offspring of two siblings.

The number in front of the word *cousin* corresponds to going another generation down both sides of the family tree; for example, the grandparents of second cousins would be siblings. These are considered whole cousins.

If two people are not descended by the same number of generations from siblings, count the number of steps "removed" between them, and you will have the exact kinship. For example, the relationship between two persons, one descended two generations from a sibling and the other three generations from the other sibling, would be second cousins, once removed (one person would be the grandchild of one of the siblings, and the other a great-grandchild of the other sibling).

More confusion . . .

Great signifies being one generation removed from the relative specified; it is often used in combination, for example, great-granddaughter.

Collateral lineage is when two people have a common ancestor, but neither one is an ancestor of the other.

Fictive kinship is a relationship, such as with a godparent, modeled on relations of kinship but created by customary convention rather than the circumstances of birth.

Consanguinity is relationship by blood (i.e., presumed biological) ties. A consanguine is a relative by birth, as distinguished from an in-law ("affine") or step-relative.

Affinity is relationship by marriage ties. Whenever the connection between two relatives includes one or more marital links, the two have no necessary biological relationship and are classed as an affinal relative, or affine.

ORDER UP!

According to most accounts, the Fourth Earl of Sandwich, John Montagu, invented the tasty concoction the world now so enjoys—the sandwich. But what drove him to such a brilliant brainstorm? The most popular story, most likely false, places him at a marathon poker game in 1762. Unwilling to miss a single hand, he sent his valet off to concoct the original sandwich with what was available in the larder: a piece of salt beef between two slices of toasted bread. But the more likely story, according to the earl's biographer, N.A.M. Rodger, places Montagu at sea. Needing a portable meal, he put a piece of meat between two slices of bread: hence, the sandwich!

LETTERS FROM THE PAST

Words like *encyclopedia* are occasionally spelled *encyclopaedia*, a throwback to old English, when the letter called *ash* (a and e together) was still part of the alphabet. Another vestige of old English is found in signs saying "Ye Olde..."—the letter called *thorn*, which made a th sound, looked similar to the modern y in handwriting.

METALLIC COMBINATIONS

An alloy is a combination of two or more elements, at least one of which is a metal (usually both are), and where the resultant material has metallic properties.

Alloys of Aluminum

Al-Li = aluminum + lithium
Alumel = aluminum + nickel
Duralumin = aluminum + copper + manganese + magnesium
Magnox = aluminum + magnesium oxide

Alloys of Potassium

NaK = potassium + sodium

Alloys of Iron

Steel = iron + carbon
Stainless steel = iron + chromium + nickel
Surgical stainless steel = iron + chromium + molybdenum
  + nickel
Silicon steel = iron + silicon
Tool steel = iron + tungsten *or* iron + manganese
Cast iron = iron + carbon (smaller amount of carbon than
  in steel)
Spiegeleisen = iron + manganese + carbon

Alloys of Cobalt

Stellite = cobalt + chromium + tungsten + carbon
Talonite = cobalt + chromium

Alloys of Silver

Sterling silver = silver + copper

Alloys of Nickel

German silver = nickel + copper + zinc
Chromel = nickel + chromium
Mu-metal = nickel + iron
Monel metal = nickel + copper + iron + manganese
Nichrome = nickel + chromium + iron
Nicrosil = nickel + chromium + silicon + magnesium
Nisil = nickel + silicon + magnesium

Alloys of Copper

Brass = copper + zinc
Constantan = copper + nickel
Prince's metal = copper + zinc
Gilding metal = copper + zinc
Bronze = copper + tin, aluminum, or any other element
Phosphor bronze = copper + tin + phosphorus
Bell metal = copper + tin
Beryllium copper = copper + beryllium
Cupronickel = copper + nickel
Nickel silver = copper + nickel
Billon = copper + silver
Nordic gold = copper + aluminum + zinc + tin

Alloys of Tin

Pewter = tin + lead + copper
Solder = tin + lead

Rare Earth Alloys

Misch metal = cerium + lanthanum + various traces

Alloys of Gold

Electrum = gold + silver
18K gold = 18 parts gold + 6 parts another metal
   (75 percent gold)
14K gold = 14 parts gold + 10 parts another metal
   (58.3 percent gold)
12K gold = 12 parts gold + 12 parts another metal
   (50 percent gold)
10K gold = 10 parts gold + 14 parts another metal
   (41.7 percent gold)

(Other metals present in gold alloys allow jewelers to vary the color; nickel, palladium, copper, and silver are some of those used.)

Alloys of Mercury

Amalgam = mercury + silver *or* mercury + tin

Alloys of Lead

Solder = lead + tin
Terne = lead + tin (ratio differs from that in solder)
Type metal = lead + tin + antimony

◆

DID HE GO TO BURGER KING?

"Elvis has left the building" was the message actually used over PA systems after the King's concerts, in the hope that it would persuade people to go home.

THE RICHTER EARTHQUAKE SCALE

In 1935, American seismologist Charles F. Richter created a scale to measure how much the ground shakes during an earthquake. On the Richter Scale, magnitudes increase logarithmically: energy increases tenfold with each magnitude number.

Descriptor	Magnitude	Effects	Estimated Frequency
Micro	<2.0	Microearthquakes, recorded, but not felt	8,000 per day
Very minor	2.0–2.9	Generally not felt, but recorded	1,000 per day
Minor	3.0–3.9	Often felt; rarely cause damage	49,000 per year
Light	4.0–4.9	Rattling indoor items; noises	6,200 per year
Moderate	5.0–5.9	Slight damage to buildings	800 per year
Strong	6.0–6.9	Destruction in 100-mile radius	120 per year
Major	7.0–7.9	Serious damage over larger areas	18 per year
Great	8.0–8.9	Serious damage over a diameter of more than 500 miles	1 per year
Rare great	>9.0	Major damage over 1,000 miles	1 per 20 years

FROM BAD TO WORSE

The Saffir/Simpson Hurricane Scale is based on a hurricane's intensity.

Category	Wind Speed (mph)	Storm Surge (wave footage)	Damage
1	74–95	4–5	Minor
2	96–110	6–8	Moderate
3	111–130	9–12	Major
4	131–155	13–18	Severe
5	> 155	> 18	Catastrophic

COURTSIDE MAGIC

One of the least understood occupations in plain view of the public is the court reporter. What are they doing with that weird typewriter? How could anyone type anything with so few keys?

The shorthand machine has come a long way since the first modern version was developed in Ireland by Miles Bartholemew in 1879. Later improvements made by Americans led to the modern stenographic machine which became common after World War II. The key to the amazing speed at which a machine stenographer could record speech was the limited number of keys on the shorthand machine's keyboard. Some less common letters are recorded by pressing more than one key at a time, thus cutting down on hand movement. Also, machine stenography, like shorthand, frequently breaks words down into syllables, rather than letters.

Today, computer aided transcription (CAT) devices have replaced the old shorthand machines and have taken court reporting to a new level of speed and simplicity.

MOODY BLUES . . . AND GREENS

While mood rings don't really reflect your mood with scientific accuracy, some say they are reliable indicators of your body's involuntary physical reactions. The stone in a mood ring has thermotropic liquid crystals that change according to changes in the temperature in your hand, and thus change the color of the crystals:

Dark blue: Happy, romantic, or passionate
Blue: Calm or relaxed
Blue-green: Somewhat relaxed
Green: Normal
Amber: A little nervous or anxious
Gray: Very nervous or anxious
Black: Stressed

◆

DISORIENTATION

The Möbius strip is what's known as a nonorientable surface—it has only one side and one edge. This circular conundrum is named after August Ferdinand Möbius, a nineteenth-century German mathematician and astronomer. You can build one with a strip of paper, making a half twist and taping the ends together. (If you're the suspicious sort, paint each side of the paper a different color before taping it.) Its usefulness? Well, picture this: Möbius strips were commonly used as car fan belts, as both sides are utilized equally, therefore halving the wear and tear. Today, the majority of cars have a regular loop fan belt; some say this is planned obsolescence.

THE DOW-RE-MI

In 1896, Charles Dow created the Dow Jones Industrial
Average (DJIA) with just twelve stocks:

1. American Cotton Oil
2. American Sugar Refining Co.
3. American Tobacco
4. Chicago Gas
5. Distilling & Cattle Feeding Co.
6. General Electric Co.
7. Laclede Gas Light Co.
8. National Lead
9. North American Co.
10. Tennessee Coal, Iron & Railroad Co.
11. U.S. Leather
12. U.S. Rubber Co.

The number of stocks in the DJIA climbed to twenty in 1916,
and then to thirty in 1928, where it remains today (though the
stocks chosen for the DJIA change). General Electric is the
only one of the original twelve stocks to remain. The present
stocks are:

1. 3M Corporation
2. Alcoa
3. American International Group
4. Altria (was Philip Morris)
5. American Express
6. Boeing
7. Caterpillar
8. CitiGroup
9. Coca-Cola

10. E.I. DuPont de Nemours
11. Exxon Mobil
12. General Electric
13. General Motors
14. Hewlett-Packard
15. Home Depot
16. Honeywell
17. Intel
18. International Business Machines
19. J.P. Morgan Chase
20. Johnson & Johnson
21. McDonald's
22. Merck
23. Microsoft
24. Pfizer
25. Procter and Gamble
26. SBC Communications
27. United Technologies
28. Verizon Communications
29. Wal-Mart Stores
30. Walt Disney

THE MONASTIC HOURS

Hour of the Day	Latin Name
Midnight	Matins
3 A.M.	Lauds
6 A.M.	Prime
9 A.M.	Terce
Noon	Sext
3 P.M.	None
Sunset	Vespers
Nightfall	Compline

MR. SHERIDAN'S WRITE STUFF

Mrs. Malaprop, introduced in Richard Sheridan's 1775 play *The Rivals*, lived in an etymological world filled with colorful turns of phrase that were always just a bit off. Her mistakes arose from substituting a similar-sounding word for the word that she intended, called a malapropism, from the French phrase *mal à propos*, inappropriate. These slips are divided into two types: classical malapropisms, mistakes due to ignorance (as in the case of Mrs. Malaprop), and temporary slips of the tongue, in which the intended word is known by the speaker but has been inadvertently replaced. A related word gaffe is the *mondegreen*, which is a misheard saying or phrase. It is a sort of aural malapropism, usually used in regard to song lyrics.

A few of Mrs. Malaprop's original -isms from *The Rivals*:

"Promise to forget this fellow—to illiterate him, I say, quite from your memory." (obliterate)

"If ever you betray what you are entrusted with . . . you forfeit my malevolence for ever." (benevolence)

"She's as headstrong as an allegory on the banks of Nile." (alligator)

"I am sorry to say, Sir Anthony, that my affluence over my niece is very small." (influence)

"He is the very pine-apple of politeness!" (pinnacle)

"Why, murder's the matter! slaughter's the matter! killing's the matter!—but he can tell you the perpendiculars." (particulars)

"I have since laid Sir Anthony's preposition before her." (proposition)

SECRET STASH

The main reason for opening a Swiss bank account is nothing clandestine, merely the legendary privacy it affords. Long a haven for ordinary people around the world as well as James Bond's nemeses, Swiss banks require a minimum amount for deposit of a mere $15,000. The Swiss currently charge a hefty 35 percent tax on interest earned in their banks' accounts, but Americans, for example, can receive 30 percent of that back by showing they're not Swiss residents. Of course, then it's not a secret anymore, is it?

◆

AAAACH-HOW?

Some illnesses are viral and others bacterial. Here's a short list of what's what:

Viruses	*Bacteria*
AIDS	Botulism
Chicken pox	Diphtheria
Common cold	Gonorrhea
Encephalitis	Lyme disease
Hepatitis	Whooping cough
Herpes simplex	Scarlet fever
Mononucleosis	Syphilis
Influenza	
Measles	
Mumps	
Poliomyelitis	
German measles	
Yellow fever	

ENDANGERED

According to the United States Fish and Wildlife Service, as of 2004, the number of endangered or threatened species breaks down as follows:

Mammals	346	Flowering Plants	716
Birds	272	Conifers and Cycads	5
Fishes	126	Ferns and Allies	26
Reptiles	115	Lichens	2
Clams	72		
Insects	48	Plant Total	749
Snails	33		
Amphibians	30		
Crustaceans	21		
Arachnids	12		
Animal Total	1075	Grand Total	1824

THE TEN PLAGUES

The Old Testament speaks of ten plagues that would befall Egypt if the Pharaoh did not release the Jewish people from slavery. They are:

1. Blood
2. Frogs
3. Lice or gnats
4. Flies
5. Cattle disease
6. Boils
7. Hail
8. Locusts
9. Darkness
10. Death of the firstborn

A typical LIGHTNING BOLT is two to four inches wide and two miles long.

TAKING MEASURE
Universal Sizes of Everyday Things

Chopsticks: Chinese are blunt-ended and 10 inches long; Japanese are pointed and are 8 inches for men and 7 inches for women

Scallops: 36.3 scallop meats per pound (weighed out of shell, as per a 1982 U.S. federal regulation)

U.S. dollar bills: 6⅛ inches by 2⅝ inches (any denomination) . . . and speaking of money, a quarter is about 1 inch, and a penny ¾ inch

Standard linoleum tiles: 12 inches square

Credit card: 3⅜ inches by 2⅛ inches

Residential plumbing pipe: ⅛ inch smaller than outside diameter

Most business cards: 3½ inches by 2 inches

Marbles: Shooter is between ½ inch and ¾ inch; target is ⅝ inch

Pizza: The European Union Traditional Pizza Association insists that crust diameter not exceed 30 centimeters

Badminton shuttlecock: 14 to 16 feathers, 4.74 to 5.5 grams

Osprey nesting site: 4-foot by 4-foot platform, 15 to 20 feet high, ½ mile apart from one another

Napkins: Cloth, dinner, 16 to 18 inches unfolded; cloth, cocktail, 10 to 12 inches unfolded; cocktail, paper, 9½ inches

Threaded handles: Brooms, paint rollers, extension poles for window-washing brushes, and squeegees have universal threading—¾ inch in diameter, 5 threads per inch

Sari: 4 feet wide, 12 to 27 feet long

FEELING FRIGHTENED?
Seems Like Everybody's Afraid of Something

Aerophobia: Fear of swallowing air
Anemophobia: Fear of wind
Anthrophobia: Fear of flowers
Arachibutyrophobia: Fear of peanut butter sticking to the roof of the mouth
Aulophobia: Fear of flutes
Barophobia: Fear of gravity
Bibliophobia: Fear of books
Blennophobia: Fear of slime
Chaetophobia: Fear of hair
Chronophobia: Fear of time
Clinicophobia: Fear of going to bed
Deciophobia: Fear of making decisions
Dendrophobia: Fear of trees
Eleutherophobia: Fear of freedom
Eosophobia: Fear of daylight
Epistemophobia: Fear of knowledge
Ergophobia: Fear of work
Geliophobia: Fear of laughter
Geniophobia: Fear of chins
Genuphobia: Fear of knees
Geumaphobia: Fear of taste
Helmintophobia: Fear of being infested with worms
Hippopotomonstrosesquippedaliophobia: Fear of long words
Linonophobia: Fear of string
Melophobia: Fear of music
Metrophobia: Fear of poetry
Nebulaphobia: Fear of fog
Ophthalmophobia: Fear of opening one's eyes

Ostraconophobia: Fear of shellfish
Papyrophobia: Fear of paper
Pentheraphobia: Fear of mothers-in-law
Phobophobia: Fear of fear
Phronemophobia: Fear of thinking
Sophophobia: Fear of learning
Stasibasiphobia: Fear of walking
Thaasophobia: Fear of sitting
Triskadekaphobia: Fear of the number 13
Xanthophobia: Fear of the color yellow

THE TARTAN

The use of tartans by Scottish clans is quite new, historically speaking. Few precede the Jacobite uprising of 1745, and most belong to regions rather than specific families. Dress at that time often also signified rank and status; for example, servants wore clothes of only one color, rent-paying farmers used two colors, and so on, all the way up to seven colors for a king's wardrobe.

In Scotland, the word *tartan* is used to describe cross-checked fabric. Plaid describes a primitive garment, originally made by sewing together two twenty-seven-inch widths of hand-woven tartan cloth, each twelve feet long, for a five-foot by seven-foot garment or blanket. The design of a tartan is formed by an arrangement of colored stripes in the warp (length) and weft (threads across the width of cloth). It becomes a tartan when two sets of threads are interwoven at right angles. Most tartans are a mirror repeat—one half of the design is the exact reverse of the other.

ART FROM THE SEA

Scrimshaw is an indigenous American craft adopted by American whalers in the early 1800s who were frequently at sea for up to four or five years. In their monotony, whalers turned to etching and carving parts of their catch, such as the teeth, jawbones, or baleen of the whale; these valuable whale parts were often part of their pay, and later they would use them as barter with shopkeepers in port.

Scrimshanders etched their designs into the piece with sailing needles or knives—whaling scenes, ships, and women were popular subjects—which were then covered with India ink brought on board by the whalers. The surface was then rubbed with a cloth, which left ink in the etched areas. The origin of the word is obscure; one interesting etymology is a Dutch phrase meaning "to waste one's time." Today, artisans use plastics; any ivory used in the United States has been reduced to "pre-embargo ivory," which was brought into the states before sanctions were set in place.

◆

THAT IS SO HARD
The Mohs Scale for Mineral Hardness

Devised by Frederich Mohs (1773–1839), a German mineralogist, the Mohs scale is a relatively arbitrary ranking of hardness for a selection of widely available substances.

1. Talc
2. Gypsum
3. Calcite
4. Fluorite
5. Apatite

6. Orthoclase
7. Quartz
8. Topaz
9. Corundum
10. Diamond

BUT, OFFICER . . .

The following are actual statements to insurance companies offered by drivers involved in auto accidents:

The guy was all over the road. I had to swerve a number of times before I hit him.

An invisible car came out of nowhere, struck my car, and vanished.

I pulled away from the side of the road, glanced at my mother-in-law, and headed over the embankment.

In an attempt to kill a fly, I drove into a telephone pole.

I collided with a stationary truck coming the other way.

My car was legally parked as it backed into the other vehicle.

I told the police I was not injured, but on removing my hat, found that I had a fractured skull.

The guy had no idea which way to run, so I ran over him.

I was sure the old fellow would never make it to the other side of the road when I struck him.

The telephone pole was approaching. I was attempting to swerve out of its way when it struck the front end.

A pedestrian hit me and went under my car.

I saw a slow-moving, sad-faced old gentlemen as he bounced off the hood of my car.

I had been driving for forty years when I fell asleep at the wheel and had an accident.

HERE COMES THAT SOUND AGAIN

What is a musical instrument that has no strings, pipes, frets, or keys, and that you don't touch to play? It's the Theremin, invented in 1919 by Russian scientist Léon Theremin. The instrument consists of a box with two projecting radio antennas around which the user moves his or her hands to play. The Theremin is considered to be an early precursor to the electronic synthesizer. It produces an unforgettably eerie sound that became extremely popular in experimental music and film circles in the 1950s and 1960s—the Beach Boys' "Good Vibrations" and science fiction films, most notably *The Day the Earth Stood Still,* are probably the best-remembered examples. Though many consider it nothing more than a novelty, there are kits for sale and even an occasional Theremin festival for aficionados.

HOW HOT IS HOT?

What it feels like inside your washing machine . . .

Hot: 140–160°F	Medium: 100–140°F
Warm: 80–120°F	Cool: 60–80°F

◆

CHEFS' TOQUES date back as far as the sixteenth century, but it wasn't until the mid-1800s that Marie-Antoine Carême redesigned chefs' uniforms and decided that the hats should be different sizes to distinguish the mighty from the sous: tall hats for the chefs, caps for the cooks. The folded pleats of a toque—usually more than a hundred—are said to indicate the number of ways in which a chef can cook an egg.

DISASTROUS
Fatalities of the United States' Biggest Epidemics

SPANISH INFLUENZA
Killed 500,000 in 8 months during 1918.

YELLOW FEVER
Killed more than 13,000 in 1878 in the Mississippi Valley.

AIDS
Reported toll is more than 500,000 people since 1981.

◆

CHOPSTICKS, MUSICAL AND OTHERWISE

The use of chopsticks to eat food began more than five thousand years ago, when the Chinese would take their food from the fire using sticks or branches broken from trees. Later, people began to cut food into smaller pieces so they could eat individually and because the smaller portions cooked faster. Chopsticks became the utensil of choice. Today, Japan is the only country that uses chopsticks as its only utensil.

"Chopsticks"—the piano piece—was written by a sixteen-year-old girl named Euphonia Allen, who published it under the name of Arthur de Lulli. The song's title comes not from the Asian eating utensils but from the young composer's sheet music instructions: "Play with both hands turned sideways, the little fingers lowest, so that the movements of the hands imitates the chopping from which this waltz gets its name." Sadly, Euphonia—or rather, Arthur—never wrote another song.

WORTH WAITING FOR
Interesting Exports and Where They Come From

Afghanistan: Opium, precious gems
Antigua and Barbuda: Live animals
Armenia: Brandy
Australia: Coal
Bahamas: Crawfish
Bangladesh: Jute, frozen fish
Bhutan: Electricity (to India), cardamom, cement
British Virgin Islands: Sand
Cape Verde: Shoes
Cayman Islands: Turtle products
Chad: Gum arabic, cattle
China: Sporting goods
Comoros: Ylang-ylang, vanilla, cloves
Democratic Republic of the Congo: Cobalt
Costa Rica: Electronic components
Côte d'Ivoire: Tropical woods
Cyprus: Potatoes, grapes, wine
Denmark: Ships, windmills
Dominican Republic: Ferronickel
East Timor: Sandalwood
Ecuador: Shrimp, cut flowers
El Salvador: Electricity
Eritea: Livestock, sorghum
Ethiopia: Qat
Fiji: Molasses
France: Pharmaceutical products
Gabon: Uranium
Georgia: Grapes, tea
Grenada: Nutmeg, mace
Iceland: Diatomite, ferrosilicon

Indonesia: Plywood
Ireland: Computers
Israel: Software
Jordan: Potash
Kiribati: Seaweed
Kyrgyzstan: Hydropower
Laos: Tin
Lesotho: Wool and mohair
Liechtenstein: Dental products, stamps
Luxembourg: Glass
Marshall Islands: Copra cake
Micronesia: Black pepper
Mongolia: Cashmere, fluorspar
Mozambique: Prawns, cashews
Namibia: Karakul skins
Niger: Cowpeas, onions
Papua New Guinea: Logs
Portugal: Cork
Qatar: Steel
St. Vincent and the Grenadines: Eddoes and dasheen,
                              tennis racquets
Samoa: Beer
Seychelles: Cinnamon bark
Sierra Leone: Rutile
Somalia: Charcoal, scrap metal
South Africa: Platinum
South Korea: Ships
Swaziland: Soft-drink concentrates, refrigerators
Tonga: Squash
Tunisia: Hydrocarbons
Turks and Caicos Islands: Conch shells
United Arab Emirates: Dried fish, dates
Vanuatu: Kava

Leonardo da Vinci's MONA LISA is a mere 2'6½" by 1'8⅞".
Modern technology has revealed there are three different
versions of the painting under the visible one.

BURNING CALORIES

According to the National Heart, Lung, and Blood Institute
(U.S.A.), even everyday activities burn a surprising number of
calories per hour (estimated for a 150-lb. person):

Dancing	370
Gardening	324
Office Work	240
Light Cleaning	240
Playing with Kids	216
Strolling	206
Vacuuming	150
Sitting	81
Watching TV	72
Sleeping	45

THE BEATLES hold the record for the greatest number of
recordings sold in the United States at 166.5 million. Elvis
Presley holds the number two position with 117.5 million
recordings sold.

HONEY is the only natural food that doesn't spoil. The
nectar brought to the hive by the bees is about 60 percent
water, and they "cure" it to less than 20 percent water. With a
pH of 3–4, it can last for centuries.

MASTERS OF THE HOUSE

The Bauhaus (1919–1933) motto was "Art and technology—a new unity." Founded by Walter Gropius, the school included these other original Bauhaus masters:

Josef Albers * Herbert Bayer * Marcel Breuer * Lyonel Feininger * Johannes Itten * Wassily Kandinsky * Paul Klee * Hannes Meyer * Mies van der Rohe * Laszlo Moholy-Nagy * Georg Muche * Oskar Schlemmer

◆

LAST WORDS TO LIVE BY

Popular advice on "How to Stay Young" from Baseball Hall-of-Famer Satchel Paige, later inscribed on his tombstone:

1. Avoid fried meats which angry up the blood.
2. If your stomach disputes you, lie down and pacify it with cool thoughts.
3. Keep the juices flowing by jangling around gently as you move.
4. Go very light in the vices, such as carrying on in society. The social ramble ain't restful.
5. Avoid running at all times.
6. Don't look back. Something might be gaining on you.

◆

A GOLDFISH is the only animal that is known to be able to see in both the ultraviolet and infrared light frequencies.

COMPARISON OF DIAMOND AND DIAMOND SYNTHETICS

Stone	Hardness (Mohs scale)	Degree of Dispersion (color refraction through facets)
Diamond	10 (hardest known natural substance)	High; lots of fire and liveliness
Strontium titanate (Fabulite or "Wellington")	5–6 (soft)	Too high; lots of blue flashes
Cubic zirconia (CZ)	8.5 (hard)	Very high; lots of life
Gadolinium gallium garnet (GGG, synthetic)	6.5 (somewhat soft)	High; almost identical to diamond
Yttrium aluminum garnet (YAG, synthetic)	8.5 (hard)	Very low; almost no fire
Synthetic rutile (shows yellowish color)	6.5 (soft)	Extremely high; strong yellow flashes
Zircon	7.5 (moderately hard)	Good; lively
Synthetic sapphire	9 (very hard)	Very low; little life

1 = soft; 10 = hard.

Stone	Hardness (Mohs scale)	Degree of Dispersion (color refraction through facets)
Synthetic spinel	8 (hard)	Low; little life
Glass	5–6.5 (soft)	Variable—low to good depending on cut quality

ANIMAL ONOMATOPOEIA

The sound of the word imitates the animal it's describing:

Bee: "Buzz"
Cat: "Meow"
Chickadee: "Chickadee"
Chicken: "Cluck"
Rooster: "Cockadoodledoo"
Cow: "Moo"
Crow or raven: "Caw"
Dog: "Woof" or "Grr"
Duck: "Quack"

Frog: "Ribbit"
Lion: "Roar"
Humans: "Prattle," "blab," and "brouhaha"
Mouse: "Squeak"
Owl: "Hoo"
Road runner: "Beep beep"
Pig: "Oink"
Sheep: "Baa"

ANTARCTICA is the only continent that doesn't have ants. That's ANTarctica.

The relationship between Matt Groening's mysteriously identical fez-wearing comic strip characters AKBAR AND JEFF was finally revealed to be "lovers or brothers or both."

MORSE CODE
Complete with the Radio Alphabet

A	Alpha	. -
B	Bravo	- . . .
C	Charlie	- . - .
D	Delta	- . .
E	Echo	.
F	Foxtrot	. . . - .
G	Golf	- - .
H	Hotel	. . . .
I	India	. .
J	Juliet	. - - -
K	Kilo	- . -
L	Lima	. - . .
M	Mike	- -
N	November	- .
O	Oscar	- - -
P	Papa	. - - .
Q	Quebec	- - . -
R	Romeo	. - .
S	Sierra	. . .
T	Tango	-
U	Uniform	. . -
V	Victor	. . . -
W	Whiskey	. - -
X	X-ray	- . . -
Y	Yankee	- . - -
Z	Zulu	- - . .
0		- - - - -
1		. - - - -
2		. . - - -
3		. . . - -

4	. . . . -
5	. . . . .
6	- . . . .
7	- - . . .
8	- - - . .
9	- - - - .
Period	. - . - . -
Comma	- - . . - -
Question mark	. . - - . .
Semicolon	- . - . - .
Colon	- - - . . .
Hyphen	- . . . -
Apostrophe	. - - - - .

◆

NEON NOTATIONS

Neon signage is most often neon or argon gas in a vacuum tube.

The neon sign is attributed to Georges Claude, who popularized it in Paris in 1910.

Neon signage came to America when Earle C. Anthony bought two signs for $2,400 in Paris and installed them in his Los Angeles Packard dealership.

Neon gas is fiery orange-red; argon is soft lavender; argon gas enhanced with mercury is brilliant blue.

The smaller the diameter of the tube, the more intense the light produced and the higher the voltage required.

More than 150 colors can be achieved by combining different gases (including krypton, xenon, and helium) and phosphors that coat the inside of the glass tube.

DEATH ROW MENU

ANTHONY FUENTES (NOVEMBER 2004):
Fried chicken with biscuits and jalapeño peppers, steak and
French fries, fajita tacos, pizza, a hamburger, water, and Coca-Cola

FRANK RAY CHANDLER (NOVEMBER 2004):
A Pizza Hut thin-crust medium pizza topped with
extra cheese, pepperoni, ham, Canadian taco, mushrooms,
and black olives served with iced milk

FREDERICK PATRICK McWILLIAMS (SEPTEMBER 2004):
Six fried chicken breasts with ketchup, French fries, six-layer
lasagna (ground chicken, beef, cheese, minced tomatoes,
noodles, and sauteed onions), six egg rolls, shrimp fried rice
and soy sauce, six chimichangas with melted cheese and salsa,
six slices of turkey with liver and gizzard dressing, dirty rice,
cranberry sauce, and six lemonades with extra sugar

DEMARCO MARKEITH McCULLUM (NOVEMBER 2004):
A big cheeseburger, lots of French fries, three Cokes,
apple pie, and five mint sticks

ROBERT WALKER (NOVEMBER 2004):
Ten pieces of fried chicken (leg quarters), two double-meat,
double cheeseburgers with sliced onions, pickles, tomatoes,
mayonnaise, ketchup, salt, pepper, and lettuce, one small chef
salad with chopped ham and thousand island dressing, one

large order of French fries cooked with onions, five big
buttermilk biscuits with butter, four jalapeño peppers, two
Sprites, two Cokes, one pint of rocky road ice cream, and one
bowl of peach cobbler or apple pie

LORENZO MORRIS (NOVEMBER 2004):
Fried chicken and fried fish, French bread, hot peppers, apple
pie, butter pecan ice cream, two soft drinks, either Sprites or
Big Reds, and a pack of Camel cigarettes and matches. The
request for the Camels was denied.

DOMINIQUE GREEN (OCTOBER 2004):
No final meal request

CHARLES WESLEY ROACHE (OCTOBER 2004):
Sirloin steak, popcorn shrimp, salad with blue cheese dressing,
a honey bun, and vanilla Coke

RICKY MORROW (OCTOBER 2004):
A cheeseburger, French fries, onion rings, and iced tea

ADREMY DENNIS (OCTOBER 2004):
Chef salad with French/ranch dressing, fried chicken breasts
and legs, French fries, a cheeseburger, chocolate cake, deviled
eggs, and biscuits and gravy

TONY WALKER (SEPTEMBER 2002):
French fries, five pieces of fried chicken, three Dr Peppers

RAN SHAMBURGER (SEPTEMBER 2002):
Nachos with chili and cheese, one bowl of sliced jalapeños, one bowl of picante sauce, two large onions (sliced and grilled), tacos (with fresh tomatoes, lettuce, and cheese), and toasted corn tortilla shells

T. J. JONES (AUGUST 2002):
Triple-meat cheeseburger with fried bun and everything, French fries, ketchup, four pieces of chicken (two legs, two thighs), and one fried pork-chop sandwich

STANLEY BAKER JR. (MAY 2002):
Two sixteen-ounce rib eyes, one pound turkey breast (sliced thin), twelve strips of bacon, two large hamburgers with mayonnaise, onion, and lettuce, two large baked potatoes with butter, sour cream, cheese, and chives, four slices of cheese or one-half pound of grated cheddar cheese, chef salad with blue cheese dressing, two ears of corn on the cob, one pint of mint chocolate ice cream, and four vanilla Cokes

WALTER MICKENS (JUNE 2002):
Baked chicken, rice, and carrots

DANIEL RENEAU (JUNE 2002):
French fries with salt and ketchup, one tray of nachos with cheese and jalapeños, one cheeseburger with mustard and everything, and one pitcher of sweet tea

RONFORD STYRON (MAY 2002):

Mexican platter with all the works, two Classic Cokes, pickles, olives, and cookies and cream ice cream

LESLIE DALE MARTIN (MAY 2002):

Boiled crawfish, crawfish stew, garden salad, cookies, and chocolate milk

---

DOWNRIGHT BALMY

The highest temperatures ever recorded on each continent:

Continent	Temperature (°F)	Location
Africa	136	Libya
N. America	134	California
Asia	129	Israel
Australia	128	Queensland
Europe	122	Spain
S. America	120	Argentina
Antarctica	59	Scott Coast

MOTHER GOOSE'S DAYS OF BIRTH:

Monday: Fair of face
Tuesday: Full of grace
Wednesday: Full of woe
Thursday: Has far to go
Friday: Loving and giving
Saturday: Works hard for
a living
Sunday: Bonny and blithe,
good and gay

POETIC FEET

There are five different rhythmic groups of syllables that can make up a unit of verse:

Anapestic:	Two unaccented + one accented
Dactylic:	One accented + two unaccented
Iambic:	One unaccented + one accented
Spondaic:	Two accented
Trochaic:	One accented + one unaccented
Pyrrhic:	Two unaccented

Each of these units is called a "foot," and any poet who doesn't know it won't have a leg to stand on.

◆

POETIC LINE LENGTH

The names for the number of feet within a line of poetry:

Monometer:	One foot
Dimeter:	Two feet
Trimeter:	Three feet
Tetrameter:	Four feet
Pentameter:	Five feet
Hexameter:	Six feet
Heptameter:	Seven feet
Octameter:	Eight feet

For example, Shakespeare's most popularly used poetic verse is iambic pentameter—five feet, each with one unaccented and one accented syllable.

INTERNATIONAL DAY OF PANCAKES

In England, Shrove Tuesday (the last Tuesday before the start of Lent, when Mardi Gras is also celebrated, especially in parts of the United States and Canada that have a strong French influence) is best known for the Pancake Day Race at Olney in Buckinghamshire. It has been held continuously since 1445 and remains much unchanged. The race came about after a woman cooking pancakes heard the shriving bell summoning her to confession. She ran to church wearing her apron and still holding her frying pan, and thus inspired a tradition that has lasted for more than five centuries. Under the current rules, only women wearing a dress (no slacks, no jeans), an apron, and a hat or scarf may take part in the race. Each contestant has a frying pan containing a hot, cooking pancake. She must toss it three times—causing it to land back in the pan each time—during the race. The first woman to complete the winding 375-meter course and arrive at the church, serve her pancake to the bellringer, and receive a kiss from him is the winner. She also receives a prayer book from the vicar. The record, by the way, is 63 seconds, set in 1967.

WORLD MOTOR VEHICLE PRODUCTION

In 2003, the top ten countries in the world for manufacturing automobiles were:

1. United States
2. Japan
3. Germany
4. China
5. France
6. South Korea
7. Spain
8. Canada
9. Brazil
10. United Kingdom

A GOOD TIP

Some advice on what's expected in various situations:

Airports
Skycaps: $1 per bag
Wheelchair attendant: $3–5
Electric cart driver: $2

Casinos
Blackjack dealer: $5 per session
Waitress: $1 per drink
Slot machine manager: $1 per session

Tow truck
Jump: $3–5
Tow: $5
Locked out: $5–10

Others who generally receive a tip:
DJ: $1 per song; $5 if it has to be the next song
Buffet-style restaurant waiter: 5–10%
Exotic dancer: $3 per song per person
Dog groomer: $2 per dog, or 15%
Limo driver: $20
Massage therapist: 10–20%
Cruise cabin steward: $3 per day

Holiday Tipping

Babysitter: Two nights' pay
Day care: $15–25 plus a gift
Garbage collector: $15–20
Trainer: $50
Cleaning person: One week's pay

International Eating and Drinking Tips

Canada: The tip range is 10–20 percent and is expected for restaurants, bars, food delivery, and taxis. If service is bad, it's fine not to tip at all.

China: No tipping.

France: In restaurants, a service charge is included in the price by law. It is usually about 15 percent or so. Tip about the same in bars.

Italy: Not expected in restaurants; leave some change on the table if you like.

Japan: No tipping.

Mexico: Tipping is expected for almost every service; pay is so scant that what people make in tips is truly part of their salary.

United Kingdom: No tipping in a bar or pub; buy a drink for the barkeep's service, if you like.

And one last international tipping tip: tip no one in New Zealand and Australia; tip everyone in South Africa.

◆

In 1969, MIDNIGHT COWBOY became the first and only X-rated production to win the Academy Award for Best Picture. Its rating has since been changed to R.

◆

Ten inches of SNOW equals one inch of rain in water content.

IT'S DIFFERENT FOR GIRLS

Rules have never been the same for girls and boys . . .

The Girl Scout Law

I will do my best to be
honest and fair,
friendly and helpful,
considerate and caring,
courageous and strong, and
responsible for what I say and do,
and to
respect myself and others,
respect authority,
use resources wisely,
make the world a better place, and
be a sister to every Girl Scout.

The Boy Scout Law

The Boy Scout Law varies from country to country. Here are a few different versions:

United States: A Scout is: Trustworthy, Loyal, Helpful, Friendly, Courteous, Kind, Obedient, Cheerful, Thrifty, Brave, Clean, Reverent.

South Africa: A Scout's honor is to be trusted. A Scout is loyal. A Scout's duty is to be useful and to help others. A Scout is a friend to all and a brother to every other Scout. A Scout is courteous. A Scout is a friend to animals. A Scout obeys orders. A Scout smiles and whistles under all difficulties. A Scout is thrifty. A Scout is clean in thought, word and deed.

Thailand: A Scout's honor is to be trusted. A Scout is loyal to his Nation, his Religion, his King and is faithful to his benefactors. A Scout's duty is to be useful and to help others. A Scout is a friend to all, and a brother to every other Scout in the world. A Scout is courteous. A Scout is kind to animals. A Scout respectfully obeys the orders of his parents and his superiors. A Scout is very cheerful and is not afraid of troubles. A Scout is thrifty. A Scout is clean in thought, word and deed.

France: A Scout's honor is to be trusted. A Scout is loyal for life. A Scout's duty is to be useful and to help others. A Scout shares with everyone. A Scout is courteous and fights against injustice. A Scout protects life because it was created by God. A Scout obeys and finishes what he starts. A Scout smiles under all difficulties. A Scout is careful of possessions and property. A Scout is pure and shines pureness.

China: Honesty, Loyalty and Filial Devotion, Helpfulness, Loving Kindness, Courtesy, Justice, Responsibility, Cheerfulness, Industriousness and Thrift, Courage, Cleanness, Public Spirit

◆

ON FIRE

Though species of trees vary in their density, for use as firewood the energy content of the wood does not vary substantially enough to make a difference in efficacy. Availability, dryness, and a proper cut are equally important. But all things being equal, here are the top ten hardest species for your burning pleasure:

Rock elm * Shagbark hickory * White oak * Bitternut hickory * Sugar maple * Beech * Red oak * Yellow birch * Red elm * White ash

WHAT'S IN A NAME
The Most Popular Names for Towns in the United States

Town	How Many	Source/Derivation
Franklin	28	Statesman Benjamin Franklin
Madison	27	President James Madison
Clinton	26	Mainly local founders or politicians
Washington	26	President George Washington
Chester	25	English town
Greenville	24	Description
Marion	24	Revolutionary War general
Salem	24	Biblical place
Springfield	24	Description
Manchester	23	English city
Monroe	22	President James Monroe
Troy	22	Greek city
Ashland	21	Tree; home of Henry Clay
Milford	21	English town
Clayton	20	Mainly local founders or politicians
Fairfield	20	Description
Jackson	20	President Andrew Jackson
Jamestown	20	English king; personal name
Jefferson	20	President Thomas Jefferson
Newport	20	Description
Oxford	20	English city
Cleveland	19	President Grover Cleveland
Lebanon	19	Biblical place
Plymouth	19	English city

TOP TEN BRIGHTEST STARS

These are the ten brightest stars in the night sky as visible from Earth:

Name	Distance from Earth (in light years)	Constellation
Sirius	9	Canis Major
Canopus	313	Carina
Alpha Centauri	4	Centaurus
Arcturus	37	Bootes
Vega	25	Lyra
Capella	42	Auriga
Rigel	773	Orion
Procyon	11	Canis Minor
Achernar	144	Eridanus
Betelgeuse	427	Orion

THE INTERNATIONAL SPACE STATION

The following sixteen nations cooperated in the design, construction, and operation of the International Space Station:

Canada, Belgium, Brazil, Denmark, France, Italy, Japan, Netherlands, Norway, Russia, Spain, Sweden, Switzerland, United Kingdom, and the United States

◆

Air holes must be cut in the roof of an IGLOO to prevent suffocation.

MAGIC 8 BALL MESSAGES

In the late 1940s, Alabe Crafts Co. of Cincinnati, Ohio, invented a quirky item that would be the biggest prognosticator on the toy market since the Ouija board took hold in the 1880s. Herewith the prophetic answers offered up by the icosahedron (20-sided polyhedron) inside the mysterious sphere . . .

As I see it, yes.
Ask again later.
Better not tell you now.
Cannot predict now.
Concentrate and ask again.
Don't count on it.
It is certain.
It is decidedly so.
Most likely.
My reply is no.

My sources say no.
Outlook not so good.
Outlook good.
Reply hazy, try again.
Signs point to yes.
Very doubtful.
Without a doubt.
Yes.
Yes—definitely.
You may rely on it.

◆

MAGNETIC PERSONALITY

Magnetic resonance imaging (MRI) is used increasingly to diagnose various conditions, particularly those in the brain. MRI uses radio waves (safer than X-rays) to bring molecules into phase—in other words, aligns the molecules in the area being examined—and then observes the differences as the molecules "relax" or return to their various characteristic phases. The resulting changes are then captured with a computer. To see the body in three dimensions, the MRI device moves along the body and administers pulses of radio waves to each "slice" of tissue, and all these are reassembled into a three-dimensional image.

HOW HIGH?
The Ten Tallest Buildings in the World (as of 2005)

Building	Location	Stories	Height (ft)
1. Taipei 101	Taipei, Taiwan	101	1,670
2. Petronas Tower One	Kuala Lumpur, Malaysia	88	1,483
2. Petronas Tower Two	Kuala Lumpur, Malaysia	88	1,483
4. Sears Tower	Chicago, United States	110	1,450
5. Jin Mao Tower	Shanghai, China	88	1,380
6. Two International Finance Center	Hong Kong	88	1,362
7. CITIC Plaza	Guangzhou, China	80	1,283
8. Shun Hing Square	Shenzhen, China	69	1,260
9. Empire State Building	New York, United States	102	1,250
10. Central Plaza	Hong Kong	78	1,227

◆

The first flight of the WRIGHT BROTHERS was a distance less than the wingspan of a jumbo jet.

EXECUTED
U.S. Executions by State (1976–2004)

Texas	336	Utah	6
Virginia	94	Mississippi	6
Oklahoma	75	Washington	4
Missouri	61	Maryland	4
Florida	59	Pennsylvania	3
Georgia	36	Nebraska	3
North Carolina	34	Federal	3
South Carolina	32	Oregon	2
Alabama	30	Montana	2
Louisiana	27	Kentucky	2
Arkansas	26	Wyoming	1
Arizona	22	Tennessee	1
Ohio	15	New Mexico	1
Delaware	13	Idaho	1
Illinois	12	Colorado	1
Indiana	11		
Nevada	11	TOTAL EXECUTIONS:	944
California	10		

The forms of capital punishment used in the U.S. today are lethal injection, gas chamber, electrocution, firing squad, and hanging.

LETHAL INJECTION

Alabama	Florida
Arizona	Georgia
Arkansas	Idaho
California	Illinois
Colorado	Indiana
Connecticut	Kansas
Delaware	Kentucky

Louisiana
Maryland Mississippi
Missouri
Montana
Nevada
New Hampshire
New Jersey
New Mexico
New York
North Carolina
Ohio
Oklahoma
Oregon
Pennsylvania
South Carolina
South Dakota
Tennessee
Texas
Utah
U.S. military
U.S. government
Virginia
Washington
Wyoming

ELECTROCUTION
Alabama

Arkansas
Florida
llinois
Kentucky
Nebraska
Oklahoma
South Carolina
Tennessee
Virginia

LETHAL GAS
Arizona
California
Maryland
Missouri
Wyoming

HANGING
New Hampshire
Washington

FIRING SQUAD
Idaho
Oklahoma
Utah

U.S. Executions by Method (through July 2005)

Lethal injection	799	Hanging*	3
Electrocution	151	Firing squad*	2
Lethal gas	11		

* All states that used this method had lethal injection as an alternative choice.

AIN'T SUPERSTITIOUS?
What to Do to Keep Luck on Your Side

If you say good-bye to a friend on a bridge, you'll never see each other again.

Sweep trash out the door after dark and a stranger will visit.

Dropping the comb while you're combing your hair is a sign of a coming disappointment.

It's bad luck to cut your fingernails on a Friday or a Sunday.

Always eat a fish from the head toward the tail.

Never say the word *pig* while fishing at sea.

Drop a fork and a man will visit.

Ivy growing on a house protects the inhabitants from witchcraft and evil.

If you catch a falling leaf on the first day of autumn, you won't catch a cold all winter.

A dream about a lizard means you've got a secret enemy.

A wish will come true if you make it while burning onions.

It's bad luck to see an owl in the sunlight.

Use the same pencil to take a test that you used for studying for the test, and the pencil will remember the answers.

Salty soup is a sign that the cook is in love.

Sing before seven, cry before eleven.

A swan feather sewn into a husband's pillow ensures fidelity.

A yawn is a sign that danger is near.

Seeing an ambulance is very unlucky unless you pinch your nose or hold your breath until you see a black or a brown dog.

Wear a blue bead to protect yourself from witches.

◆

STARS AND STRIPES WHENEVER

In the early years of nationhood, the U.S. flag went through several permutations; in fact, many states designed their own versions of the stars and stripes. But in 1818, Congress voted to keep the number of stripes on the flag at thirteen, to honor the original colonies, and to add one star to the field for every new state. Each new star is officially added on the July 4 following a state's admission to the Union. A fairly recent American flag is rarely seen: the forty-nine-star version, flown for just one year between the time Alaska and Hawaii became states. Technically, the United States was a forty-nine-state country for just over seven months: Alaska was admitted on January 3, 1959, and Hawaii the following August 21, thus missing that year's July 4 "new flag" cutoff. Dwight D. Eisenhower was the only president to serve under the forty-nine-star American flag.

THINGS GOD MADE DURING EARTH'S SEVEN DAYS OF CREATION

1. Light, resulting in day and night
2. Sky
3. Earth and ocean, grass, herbs, and fruit trees
4. Sun, moon, and stars
5. Birds, fish, and whales
6. Cows, creeping things, wild animals, man, and woman
7. The Sabbath—God rested

GRAY SKIES

Sometimes science shows its whimsical side—witness these cloud names, which owe their beginnings to sailors, farmers, and old wives . . .

Cloud	Descriptive Name	Height	Description
Cirrus	Mares' tails	4 or more miles	Thin, feathery
Cirrocumulus	Mackerel sky	4 or more miles	Small patches of white
Cirrostratus	Bedsheet clouds	4 or more miles	Thin, white sheets
Stratus*	High fogs	0–1 mile	Low, gray blanket
Cumulus	Cauliflowers	¼–4 miles	Flat bottomed, white puffy
Cumulonimbus*	Thunderheads	¼–4 miles	Mountains of heavy, dark clouds

*Rain or snow clouds

◆

In many parts of the South, the American CIVIL WAR is still referred to as "The War of Northern Aggression."

-OF-THE-MONTH CLUBS
Just a Few Things You Can Get by Mail, Twelve Times a Year

Wine * Bacon * Books * Cookies * Meals * Fruit * Coffee *
Chocolate * Pizza * Flowers * Plants * Fruits * Jelly *
Salsa * Tea * Cheesecake * Beer * Candles * Popcorn * Pie *
Software * Cigars* Champagne

◆

THE VERMILLION GATE BRIDGE

Though the U.S. Navy would have preferred black with bright
yellow stripes for visibility in a city often swathed in fog, the
Golden Gate Bridge has been painted orange vermillion—or
"international orange"—ever since its completion. Architect
Irving Morrow selected the color to blend with the bridge's
stunning natural setting. Contrary to legend, the bridge is not
constantly painted end-to-end, nonstop; it has been painted
only twice. Presently, to avoid corrosion and meet air-quality
requirements, it sports an inorganic zinc silicate primer and an
acrylic emulsion topcoat.

◆

THE 1909-11 T206

For some, this code signifies the holy grail of baseball-card
collecting. Rarest of the T206 series is "The Flying
Dutchman," Honus Wagner, and estimates are that only 50
to 100 copies of this card exist. The last time one of these
Honus Wagner cards was sold, in 2000, it went for over $1.1
million.

Want to see one? A Honus Wagner T206 card is in the
collection of New York's Metropolitan Museum of Art.

THE BEST-SELLING
BOOKS OF ALL TIME

Title	First Published	Approximate Sales
The Bible	ca. 1450	More than 6 billion
Quotations from the Works of Chairman Mao Tse-Tung	1966	1 billion
American Spelling Book, by Noah Webster	1783	100 million
The Guinness Book of World Records	1955	90 million
The World Almanac	1868	75 million

◆

PATENTLY ABSURD?

According to the United States Patent and Trademark Office Web site, only the inventor may apply for a patent, with certain exceptions. If a person who is not the inventor applies for a patent, the patent, if it is obtained, becomes invalid. The person applying in such a case who falsely states that he or she is the inventor is also subject to criminal penalties. If the inventor is dead, the application may be made by legal representatives, that is, the administrator or executor of the estate. If the inventor is insane, the application for patent may be made by a guardian. If an inventor refuses to apply for a patent or cannot be found, a joint inventor or a person having a proprietary interest in the invention may apply on behalf of the nonsigning inventor.

MAC WORLD

Since 1968, the Big Mac, McDonald's flagship sandwich, has been sung about and scarfed down by the billions. It's universally known that its main ingredients are:

Two all-beef patties
Special sauce
Lettuce
Cheese

Pickles
Onions
Sesame seed bun

Many have tried to replicate the "special sauce." Herewith a popular copycat recipe:

½ cup mayonnaise
2 tablespoons French dressing
4 teaspoons sweet pickle relish
1 tablespoon finely minced white onions
1 teaspoon white vinegar
1 teaspoon sugar
⅛ teaspoon salt

McDonald's officially lists its secret sauce ingredients as:

Soybean oil, pickles, distilled vinegar, water, egg yolks, high fructose corn syrup, sugar, onion powder, corn syrup, spice and spice extracts, salt, xanthan gum, mustard flour, propylene glycol alginate, sodium benzoate and potassium sorbate as preservatives, mustard bran, garlic powder, hydrolyzed (corn gluten, wheat, and soy) proteins, caramel color, extractives of paprika, turmeric, calcium disodium EDTA to protect flavor.

THE DEWEY DECIMAL SYSTEM

Devised by library pioneer Melvil Dewey in the 1870s, this organizational system provides a logical structure for the organization of a library's unique collection. This classification is still used today in more than two hundred thousand libraries worldwide.

000	*Generalities*
100	*Philosophy and psychology*
200	*Religion*
300	*Social sciences*
400	*Language*
500	*Natural sciences and mathematics*
600	*Technology (Applied sciences)*
700	*The arts*
800	*Literature and rhetoric*
900	*Geography and history*

SAYS WHO?

Ventriloquism is much more than dummies and voice throwing. Its magical illusion relies on the fact that the ear is quite unreliable when it comes to pinpointing the direction of sound. Without visual cues, the accuracy is even poorer. To work, a ventriloquist must keep his mouth open only about a quarter of an inch at all times, muffling and faking word sounds that require the lips to be joined. Additional stagecraft includes gestures, eye movements, and patter to distract the audience. The dummy's "voice" must also have a different personality as well—pitch, cadence, and the voice's assumed sex and age can all be altered to confuse the viewer/listener.

ECHOES OF THE ALPS

Yodeling is a vocal art form begun in the Swiss and Austrian Alps, originally serving as a form of communication between houses and towns, and used for spreading simple messages and warnings. Though yodeling consists mostly of nonsense words that are sung primarily for the way they sound, it does have a specific form, switching rapidly from the lower alto, tenor, or bass "chest voices" to a falsetto or "high voice." The yodeler sounds syllables continuously upward until the voice breaks into an upper octave, then down again and up until the voice breaks again. This is done repeatedly and loudly, though some purists complain that acrobatics and speed play too much a part in modern yodeling. A piece will still occasionally end with a few real words, for example, *drobn auf da Alm*, which is Austrian dialect for "up there on the mountain."

GLOBAL EXHALE

In 2002, the top ten producers of carbon dioxide emissions into the atmosphere, the main cause of global warming, were:

1. United States	1568	6. Germany	229
2. China	906	7. Canada	161
3. Russia	415	8. United Kingdom	151
4. Japan	322	9. South Korea	123
5. India	280	10. Italy	122

(million metric tons carbon equivalent)

◆

HOMICIDE is the premiere cause of death of pregnant women.

LUCKY (AND SACRED) SEVEN

History and religion seem to have a predilection for the number seven . . .

Seven Days of Creation: The amount of time cited in the Bible in which God made the world

Seven Churches of Asia: Referred to by St. John in the Book of Revelation, they were located in Ephesus, Smyrna, Pergamum, Thyatira, Sardia, Philadelphia, and Laodicea

Seven Churches of Rome: The basilicas of St. John Lateran, St. Peter, St. Mary Major, St. Paul-Outside-the-Walls, St. Lawrence-Outside-the-Walls, St. Sebastian-Outside-the-Walls, and Holy Cross-in-Jerusalem

Seven Deadly Sins: Pride, covetousness, lust, anger, gluttony, envy, and sloth

Seven Names for Constantinople: By-sance, Antonia, New Rome, the town of Constantine, the Separator of the World's Parts, the Treasure of Islam, Stamboul

Seven Gifts: Wisdom, understanding, counsel, fortitude, knowledge, piety, and fear of the Lord

Seven Angels: In Arabian legend, they cool the sun with ice and snow, so the Earth will not burn up

Seven Holy Days of Obligation: Solemnity of Mary, Easter, Solemnity of the Ascension, Solemnity of the Assumption, Solemnity of All Saints, Solemnity of the Immaculate Conception, and Christmas

Seventh Son: Mythical personages often father seven sons. It is especially fortunate to be the seventh son of the seventh son.

Seven as the Age of Reason: In Christianity, seven is considered the age of reason, and the age when a child is held accountable for sins and begins confession.

Seven Sacraments: Baptism, Confirmation, the Eucharist, Penance, Holy Orders, Matrimony, and Anointing of the Sick

Seven Wedding Blessings: A special set for the bride and groom at Jewish weddings

Seven States of Purification: Egyptian dogma for the stages of the transmigration of the soul

Seven Deities: Egyptians had seven original and higher gods; the Phœnicians seven kabiris; the Persians, seven sacred horses of Mithra; the Parsees, seven angels opposed by seven demons, and seven celestial abodes paralleled by seven lower regions.

◆

WHO IS THIS EMILY, AND WHAT IS HER LIST?

She's not a woman, she's an acronym. EMILY's List stands for "Early Money Is Like Yeast" ("It makes the dough rise"), a financial network to promote pro-choice Democratic women political candidates. It was started in 1985, not by an Emily, but by Ellen R. Malcolm, a Washington, D.C., activist.

SWIM WITH CARE!

These sea creatures can be dangerous, even fatal:

Cone-Shell: A beautiful, small mollusk that lives in the South Pacific and Indian Oceans. It shoots poison barbs into its victims. For humans, they cause mild paralysis and, infrequently, death.

Octopus: All varieties of this common animal produce a paralysis-causing venom, but none is known to be fatal to humans.

Portuguese Man-of-War: This warm-water jellyfish, with tentacles up to 70 feet long, defends itself with painful stings which can cause shock, and thus be indirectly fatal to humans.

Sea Wasp: A warm-water jellyfish with 30-foot-long tentacles, whose deadly stings cause an immediate collapse of the human circulatory system.

Stingray: Although their sting is seldom fatal, an encounter with a stingray can cause vomiting, breathing difficulties, and/or gangrene.

Stonefish: Dangerous because it lies motionless in shallow South Pacific and Indian Ocean waters, a stonefish bite causes severe pain, rapid paralysis, but is only infrequently fatal.

◆

SALT is the only rock that can be eaten by humans, making it, one might say . . . worth its salt.

It is believed by some scholars that Joseph's COAT OF MANY COLORS was an early tie-dyed garment.

◆

WHAT ARE THE ODDS?

If you toss the dice, these are the chances you take . . .

Total on Dice	Odds
2	35 to 1
3	17 to 1
4	11 to 1
5	8 to 1
6	31 to 5
7	5 to 1
8	31 to 5
9	8 to 1
10	11 to 1
11	17 to 1
12	35 to 1

. . . or deal the cards and take your chances:

Poker Hand	Odds
Royal flush	649,739 to 1
Straight flush	72,192 to 1
Four of a kind	4,164 to 1
Full house	693 to 1
Flush	508 to 1
Straight	254 to 1
Three of a kind	46 to 1
Two pairs	20 to 1
One pair	2.37 to 1

REMEMBER YOUR ANNIVERSARY?

What you give and what you get has changed some over the last several decades. Parts of the traditional list of anniversary gifts, however, have existed since medieval times. The silver and golden landmarks reach back to medieval Germany, where garlands of these materials were presented as gifts for the twenty-fifth and fiftieth celebrations, respectively. Perhaps surprisingly, the "traditional" list did not exist until 1937, when the American National Retail Jeweler Association published options that included suggestions for the first fifteen years and then every five years thereafter, up to sixty. The origin of the modern list is unclear, but like the original, each year seems to be more precious and extravagant than the one before.

Anniversary	Traditional Gift	Modern Gift
First	Paper	Clocks
Second	Cotton	China
Third	Leather	Crystal/Glass
Fourth	Fruit/Flowers	Appliances
Fifth	Wood	Silverware
Sixth	Candy/Iron	Wood
Seventh	Wool/Copper	Desk Sets
Eighth	Bronze/Pottery	Linens/Lace
Ninth	Pottery/Willow	Leather
Tenth	Tin/Aluminum	Diamond Jewelry
Eleventh	Steel	Fashion Jewelry
Twelfth	Silk/Linen	Pearls
Thirteenth	Lace	Textiles/Furs
Fourteenth	Ivory	Gold Jewelry
Fifteenth	Crystal	Watches
Twentieth	China	Platinum

Anniversary	Traditional Gift	Modern Gift
Twenty-fifth	Silver	Silver
Thirtieth	Pearl	Diamond
Thirty-fifth	Coral	Jade
Fortieth	Ruby	Ruby
Forty-fifth	Sapphire	Sapphire
Fiftieth	Gold	Gold
Fifty-fifth	Emerald	Emerald
Sixtieth	Diamond	Diamond

◆

NOTHING IS AS IT SEEMS

Lettuce is from the sunflower family.

The cashew nut and poison ivy are relations.

Both apples and pears are from the rose family.

Those cute baby carrots? No such thing. They're the usual carrot, shaved down to pint-sized pieces.

◆

Q is the only letter in the alphabet that does not appear in the name of any state of the United States.

◆

TOP 10 U.S. States ranked by American Indian and Alaska Native population:

1. California
2. Oklahoma
3. Arizona
4. New Mexico
5. Texas
6. North Carolina
7. Alaska
8. Washington
9. New York
10. South Dakota

THE (EXTRA)ORDINARY OLIVE

The goddess Athena planted the first olive tree near the Acropolis, or so legend has it, and a tree that grows there today is said to have come from the seeds of the original. The olive tree is one of the most prestigious trees in history. As far back as Noah and the ark, a dove returned from the deluge with an olive branch, a sign of life; since then, the branch has also become a symbol of peace. Though it is believed that trees have been cultivated separately in both Syria and Crete as far back as 3000 B.C.E., recent carbon-dating in Spain has found an olive seed, *O. europaea*, thought to be eight thousand years old.

These days, olive oil enjoys a wide variety of uses:

- To unstick a zipper
- To silence squeaky doors
- To shine stainless steel
- As an alternate to shaving cream
- To feed to your cat as hairball prevention
- A sip before sleep to coat the throat and stop snoring
- A swallow to stop a tickle in the throat

And then there's the fruit: salty, deep, rich, and almost as varied in size as in taste. Below, a list of olive count ranges per kilogram:

Bullet (351–380)	Extra Jumbo (161–180)
Fine (321–350)	Giant (141–160)
Brilliant (291–320)	Colossal (121–140)
Superior (261–290)	Super Colossal (111–120)
Large (231–260)	Mammoth (101–110)
Extra Large (201–230)	Super Mammoth (91–100)
Jumbo (181–200)	

PETS IN THE WHITE MOUSE . . . ER, HOUSE

Just a Few of the Crawlers—Creepy and Otherwise—
Who've Lived at 1600 Pennsylvania Avenue

John Quincy Adams raised silkworms.

Aside from the expected bear, of course, Teddy Roosevelt and his clan had dogs, cats, squirrels, raccoons, rabbits, guinea pigs, a badger, a pony, a parrot, and a green garter snake.

William Howard Taft enjoyed peeking out the Oval Office window to watch Pauline Wayne, his cow, who grazed on the front lawn. Pauline was often accompanied by Enoch, her gander friend.

William McKinley often chatted with his Mexican yellow parrot.

And Andrew Johnson did, in fact, keep white mice as pets.

Other White House occupants have included zebras, coyotes, badgers, guinea pigs, hyenas, alligators, lizards, snakes, turtles, and ponies.

◆

TRULY PUZZLING

Word squares—the progenitor of the crossword puzzle—go back to ancient times; in fact, one was found in the Roman ruins of Pompeii. In nineteenth-century England, word squares had become the basis for primitive crossword puzzles for children, but adults didn't do them until *The World* newspaper's word-cross in 1913. Oddly, one of the last newspapers to hold out on what had become a worldwide craze was *The New York Times*, which did not publish a Sunday puzzle until 1942, and a daily puzzle until 1950.

ERIN McHUGH

TEA TOTALING

Though the British have made tea an integral part of their
lives for more than 350 years, the legend of the first cup of tea
dates back to 2737 B.C.E. China and the emperor Shen Nung.
A scientist and herbalist, he was sitting beneath a tree while
his servant boiled drinking water. Dried leaves dropped into
the water and the emperor decided to try the brew. The tree
was a wild tea tree.

The Duchess of Bedford is reputed to have originated the
idea of afternoon tea in the early 1800s to ward off hunger between lunch and dinner. Two tea services evolved: "high" and
"low." "Low" tea was for the wealthy and featured delicate
gourmet tidbits and sandwiches, served between 3 and 5 P.M.
"High" tea, eaten between 5 and 7 P.M., was the major meal for
the middle and lower classes, consisting of dinner items.

More tea is drunk worldwide that any other beverage
except water. India, China, Sri Lanka, Kenya, and Indonesia
account for nearly 80 percent of the world's tea production.

Top Ten Countries in World Tea Consumption (as of 1997):

Country	Percentage of World Tea Consumption
India	23
China	16
Russia/CIS	6
United Kingdom	6
Japan	5
Turkey	5
Pakistan	4
United States	4
Iran	3
Egypt	3

THE PERFECT FOOD—IN EVERY SIZE

Several things influence the size of an egg: the major factor is the age of the hen, as her eggs increase in size with her age. The breed and weight of the bird also make a difference. Lastly, heat, stress, and overcrowding will affect the size of the eggs. Consumers generally will see only medium-size eggs and larger; below are egg monikers and minimum weight per dozen (in ounces) in the United States and United Kingdom.

Peewee (15)	Large (24)
Small (18)	Extra Large (27)
Medium (21)	Jumbo (30)

◆

HOW MUCH?

What part of *one* don't you understand?

Prefix	Equivalent	Prefix	Equivalent
Atto	Quintillionth part	Deci	Tenth part
Femto	Quadrillionth part	Deka	Tenfold
Pico	Trillionth part	Hecto	Hundredfold
Nano	Billionth part	Kilo	Thousandfold
Micro	Millionth part	Mega	Millionfold
Milli	Thousandth part	Giga	Billionfold
Centi	Hundredth part	Tera	Trillionfold

WHAT'S YOUR SIGN?

The word *zodiac* comes for the Greek *zodiakos*, meaning
"circle of animal"; evidence points to the Greek scheme of
twelve zodiacal constellations appearing about 300 B.C.E. The
zodiac is an imaginary belt extending approximately 8 degrees
on either side of the Sun's apparent path, called the ecliptic. It
includes the apparent paths of the Moon and all the planets
except Pluto, whose path is eccentric. Each sign of the zodiac
is approximately 30 degrees and is an artificial division of the
Sun's path through the twelve constellations. (Libra, the
scales, by the way, is the only inanimate symbol in the zodiac.)

Sign	Symbol	Birthdates
Aries	Ram	March 21–April 19
Taurus	Bull	April 20–May 20
Gemini	Twins	May 21–June 21
Cancer	Crab	June 22–July 22
Leo	Lion	July 23–August 22
Virgo	Virgin	August 23–September 22
Libra	Scales	September 23–October 23
Scorpio	Scorpion	October 24–November 21
Sagittarius	Archer	November 22–December 21
Capricorn	Goat	December 22–January 19
Aquarius	Water	January 20–February 18
Pisces	Fish	February 19–March 20

The TREATY OF FORT JACKSON (1814) compelled
the Creek Indians to cede 23 million acres of land to the
United States, comprising about half of Alabama and part of
Georgia.

STRIPES AND SOLIDS

Everyone knows that when you're "behind the eight ball" things are looking pretty black, but here's a bit more about the color of the cue and the fifteen "object balls" around the rest of the pool table. The number, type, diameter, color, and patterns of billiard balls differ, depending on the game at hand:

1. Yellow	9. White with yellow stripe
2. Blue	10. White with blue stripe
3. Red	11. White with red stripe
4. Purple	12. White with purple stripe
5. Orange	13. White with orange stripe
6. Green	14. White with green stripe
7. Plum	15. White with plum stripe
8. Black	Cue ball: White

Eight ball, **straight pool**, and related games used all 16 balls

Nine ball uses only object balls 1 to 9
Regulation balls for these games have a 2¼" diameter and weigh 5½ to 6 ounces

Snooker uses 15 red balls, 6 colored balls (yellow, green, brown, blue, pink, and black) and one cue ball; all are unnumbered and are 2⅟₁₆" in diameter

Carom billiards uses 2 object balls and 1 cue ball on a pocketless table

◆

The photographs ANDY WARHOL used to silkscreen his 1964 *Marilyn* series are stills from her film *Niagara*.

MOST POPULAR BABY NAMES
ACROSS THE U.S. IN 2003

Boys

Alabama	William
Alaska	Jacob
Arizona	Jacob
Arkansas	Jacob
California	Daniel
Colorado	Jacob
Connecticut	Matthew
Delaware	Michael
District of Columbia	Michael
Florida	Michael
Georgia	William
Hawaii	Joshua
Idaho	Ethan
Illinois	Michael
Indiana	Jacob
Iowa	Jacob
Kansas	Ethan
Kentucky	Jacob
Louisiana	Jacob
Maine	Jacob
Maryland	Joshua
Massachusetts	Matthew
Michigan	Jacob
Minnesota	Jacob
Mississippi	William
Missouri	Jacob
Montana	Jacob
Nebraska	Jacob

Nevada	Anthony
New Hampshire	Jacob
New Jersey	Michael
New Mexico	Joshua
New York	Michael
North Carolina	Jacob
North Dakota	Ethan
Ohio	Jacob
Oklahoma	Jacob
Oregon	Jacob
Pennsylvania	Michael
Puerto Rico	Luis
Rhode Island	Michael
South Carolina	William
South Dakota	Jacob
Tennessee	William
Texas	José
Utah	Ethan
Vermont	Ethan
Virginia	Jacob
Washington	Jacob
West Virginia	Jacob
Wisconsin	Jacob
Wyoming	Jacob

TOTALS: JACOB: 25, MICHAEL: 8, ETHAN: 5, WILLIAM: 5, JOSHUA: 3, MATTHEW: 2, ANTHONY: 1, DANIEL: 1, JOSÉ: 1, LUIS: 1

Girls

Alabama	Madison
Alaska	Hannah
Arizona	Emily
Arkansas	Madison
California	Emily
Colorado	Emily
Connecticut	Emma
Delaware	Emily
District of Columbia	Kayla
Florida	Emily
Georgia	Emily
Hawaii	Emma
Idaho	Emma
Illinois	Emily
Indiana	Emma
Iowa	Emma
Kansas	Emma
Kentucky	Emily
Louisiana	Madison
Maine	Emma
Maryland	Emily
Massachusetts	Emily
Michigan	Emma
Minnesota	Emma
Mississippi	Madison
Missouri	Emma
Montana	Emma
Nebraska	Emma
Nevada	Emily
New Hampshire	Emma

New Jersey	Emily
New Mexico	Alexis
New York	Emily
North Carolina	Emma
North Dakota	Emma
Ohio	Emma
Oklahoma	Emily
Oregon	Emma
Pennsylvania	Emily
Puerto Rico	Alondra
Rhode Island	Emily
South Carolina	Madison
South Dakota	Emma
Tennessee	Madison
Texas	Emily
Utah	Emma
Vermont	Emma
Virginia	Emily
Washington	Emma
West Virginia	Madison
Wisconsin	Emma
Wyoming	Emma

TOTALS: EMMA: 23, EMILY: 18, MADISON: 7, ALEXIS: 1, ALONDRA: 1 HANNAH: 1, KAYLA: 1

Source: Social Security Administration, 2003.

◆

CONFETTI, the Italian word for "sweets," has its origins in Italian villages, where treats were thrown over the newlyweds as they left the church as a sort of fertility ritual. In poorer towns, rice, raisins, flower petals, and Jordan almonds were tossed.

WHAT WERE THEIR RANKS?
Of Forty-three American Presidents, Only Twenty-eight
Have Served in the Military

General of the Army	Dwight D. Eisenhower
	Ulysses S. Grant
Lieutenant General	George Washington
Major General	James Garfield
	William Henry Harrison
	Rutherford B. Hayes
	Andrew Jackson
	Zachary Taylor
Brigadier General	Benjamin Harrison
	Andrew Johnson
	Franklin Pierce
Quartermaster General	Chester A. Arthur
Colonel	James Madison
	Theodore Roosevelt
Lieutenant Colonel	James Monroe
Lieutenant Commander (Navy)	Gerald Ford
	Lyndon Baines Johnson
	Richard M. Nixon
Lieutenant	George H. W. Bush
	Jimmy Carter
	John F. Kennedy (Navy)
Lieutenant (National Guard)	George W. Bush
Major	William McKinley
	Harry S. Truman

Captain	Ronald Reagan
Captain (Militia)	Abraham Lincoln John Tyler
Private	James Buchanan

COLD VERSUS FLU

According to the National Institute of Allergy and Infectious Diseases, there are several symptomatic differences between the cold and flu, or for the layman, lots of different ways of feeling crummy . . .

Symptom	Cold	Flu
Fever	Rare	High (102–104°F), for 3–4 days
Headache	Rare	Prominent
Aches and pains	Slight	Usual, often severe
Fatigue, weakness	Mild	May last 2–3 weeks
Extreme exhaustion	Never	Early and prominent
Stuffy nose, sore throat	Common	Sometimes

SUBARU is the Japanese name for the constellation we know as the Pleiades, or Seven Sisters. The car's logo only shows six stars, because the Japanese constellation only contains the six brightest stars in the cluster.

MASCOTS

National Basketball Association

Atlanta Hawks	Harry the Hawk
Charlotte Bobcats	Rufus Lynx
Chicago Bulls	Da Bull
Cleveland Cavaliers	Moondog
Dallas Mavericks	Mavs Man
Denver Nuggets	Rocky the Mountain Lion
Golden State Warriors	Thunder
Houston Rockets	Clutch
Indiana Pacers	Boomer
Miami Heat	Burnie
Milwaukee Bucks	Bango
Minnesota Timberwolves	Crunch
New Jersey Nets	Sly
New Orleans Hornets	Hugo
Orlando Magic	Stuff the Magic Dragon
Philadelphia 76ers	Hip-Hop
Phoenix Suns	Gorilla
Sacramento Kings	Slamson
San Antonio Spurs	A coyote
Seattle Supersonics	Squatch
Toronto Raptors	The Raptor
Utah Jazz	A bear
Vancouver Grizzlies	Grizz
Washington Wizards	G-Wiz

The New York Knicks have no mascot.

Major League Baseball

Atlanta Braves	Rally
Anaheim Angels	Rally Monkey
Arizona Diamondbacks	Baxter D. Bobcat
Baltimore Orioles	Oriole Bird
Boston Red Sox	Wally the Green Monster
Chicago White Sox	Southpaw
Cincinnati Reds	Mr. Red and Gapper
Cleveland Indians	Slider
Colorado Rockies	Dinger
Detroit Tigers	Paws
Florida Marlins	Billy the Marlin
Houston Astros	Junction Jack
Kansas City Royals	Sluggerrr
Milwaukee Brewers	Bernie Brewer
Minnesota Twins	TC
New York Mets	Mr. Met
Oakland A's	Stomper
Philadelphia Phillies	Phillie Phanatic
Pittsburgh Pirates	Pirate Parrot
St. Louis Cardinals	Fredbird
San Diego Padres	The Swinging Friar
San Francisco Giants	Lou Seal
Seattle Mariners	Mariner Moose
Tampa Bay Devil Rays	Raymond
Texas Rangers	Rangers Captain
Toronto Blue Jays	Ace and Diamond
Washington Nationals	Screech

The L.A. Dodgers and the New York Yankees don't have mascots. The Chicago Cubs have no official mascot, but a fan called "Ronnie Woo-woo" is the team's unofficial mascot.

National Hockey League

Mighty Ducks of Anaheim	Wild Wing
Atlanta Thrashers	Thrash
Boston Bruins	Blades the Bruin
Buffalo Sabres	Sabretooth
Calgary Flames	Harvey the Hound
Carolina Hurricanes	Stormy
Chicago Blackhawks	Tommy Hawk
Colorado Avalanche	Howler
Columbus Blue Jackets	Stinger
Florida Panthers	Stanley C. Panther
Nashville Predators	Gnash
New Jersey Devils	N. J. Devil
New York Islanders	Sparky
Ottawa Senators	Spartacat
Pittsburgh Penguins	Iceburgh
San Jose Sharks	S. J. Sharkie
Tampa Bay Lightning	ThunderBug
Toronto Maple Leafs	Carlton the Bear
Vancouver Canucks	Fin
Washington Capitals	Slapshot

The remaining ten NHL teams do not have mascots.

National Football League

Arizona Cardinals	Big Red
Atlanta Falcons	Freddie the Falcon
Baltimore Ravens	Edgar, Allan, and Poe
Buffalo Bills	Buffalo Billy
Carolina Panthers	Sir Purr
Chicago Bears	Staley Da Bear

Dallas Cowboys	Rowdy
Denver Broncos	Thunder
Detroit Lions	Roary the Lion
Jacksonville Jaguars	Jaxson de Ville
Kansas City Chiefs	K. C. Wolf
Miami Dolphins	T. D.
Minnesota Vikings	Ragnar the Viking
New England Patriots	Pat Patriot
New Orleans Saints	Gumbo
Philadelphia Eagles	Swoop
San Francisco 49ers	Sourdough Sam
Tampa Bay Buccaneers	Captain Fear

GREAT (NICK)NAMES IN SPORTS

Tara "Terrorizer" Dakides (snowboarder)
George "The Iceman" Gervin (San Antonio Spurs)
Wayne "The Great One" Gretzky (New York Rangers)
Earvin "Magic" Johnson (Los Angeles Lakers)
Randy "The Big Unit" Johnson (New York Yankees)
Walter "The Big Train" Johnson (Washington Senators)
Michael "Air" Jordan (Chicago Bulls)
Karl "The Mailman" Malone (Los Angeles Lakers)
Shaquille "Shaq Attack" O'Neal (Los Angeles Lakers)
Gary "The Glove" Payton (Los Angeles Lakers)
William "The Refrigerator" Perry (Chicago Bears)
Walter "Sweetness" Payton (Chicago Bears)
Ted "Double Duty" Radcliffe (Homestead Grays)
Frank "The Big Hurt" Thomas (Chicago White Sox)
Dominique "Human Highlight Film" Wilkins
  (Atlanta Hawks)

SEXUAL HEALING?

Aphrodisiacs are substances that are thought to cause sexual excitement—but that's just the modern spin. Originally they were thought to be remedies for sexual anxiety, such as inadequate performance or infertility. Before science took over in the sexual potency department, substances that by their very nature represented birth or seeds, such as eggs or bulbs, were considered potency helpers; also considered sexual aids were foods that bore any resemblance to genitalia.

Today, science is at best skeptical about the effects of foods and other substances on the libido. Nevertheless, hope springs eternal. Believe this list of aphrodisiacs at your peril—or delight!

almond	mustard
aniseed	nutmeg
arugula	orchid bulbs
asparagus	oysters
avocado	pine nuts
bananas	pineapple
basil (sweet)	pistachio nuts
carrots	raspberries
celery	river snails
chocolate	sage
coffee	sea fennel
coriander (cilantro seed)	skink flesh
figs	Spanish fly
garlic	strawberries
ginger	truffles
gladius root	turnips
honey	vanilla
licorice	wine
musk	

Oh, and by the way, the ancients warned against "anaphro-disiacs"—items that they believed decreased potency:

dill * lentil * lettuce * rue * watercress * water lily

THE FIRST BOOK

Although it is known that books were being printed at least one hundred years before, the earliest printed and dated book is a copy of the *Diamond Sutra*. It was printed in China and is dated May 11, 868, in a colophon at the end of the book. Now safely ensconced in the British Library, it had been hidden in a sealed cave in China with forty thousand other books and manuscripts—a secret library discovered by a monk in 1900, which had been sealed for nearly nine hundred years.

The *Diamond Sutra* is simply seven pages, and was printed from carved wooden blocks. Though written in Chinese, it is a sacred Buddhist work, whose original Sanskrit title is *Vajracchedika-prajnaparamita-sutra*. The Buddha himself gave the *Diamond Sutra* its name, saying it should be called "The Diamond of Transcendent Wisdom" because "its teaching will cut like a diamond blade through worldly illusion to illuminate what is real and everlasting."

The note at the end of this tiny treasure reads, "Reverently made for universal distribution by Wang Jie on behalf of his two parents"; this does not mean that Wang Jie produced the volume, but rather that he had it made as a pious act.

It would be several hundred more years before Johannes Gutenberg invented the printing press; not until about 1454 did 180 Bibles come off his rudimentary invention.

WHAT'S IT GOING TO BE?

Old wives, opinionated people, and just plain nosy folks have had their say on pregnancy since time immemorial. Herewith some of the best of the old saws:

"Radiant" is how a pregnant woman is so often described. But if she's unusually moody as well, she's having a girl.

If a woman carries her weight in front, she's having a boy. If others can easily see the pregnancy from behind, a girl will be born.

If the mom-to-be was the more aggressive partner when the baby was conceived, the baby will be a boy. If the father took the lead, the baby's a girl.

If the numerals in the mother-to-be's age when she conceived are either both even or both odd, the baby will be a girl. If one is even and one odd, she's having a boy.

A pregnant woman dreams of a child of the opposite sex from the one she will have.

When asked to show her hands, a pregnant woman will show them with palms up for a girl and with palms down for a boy.

If the mother-to-be has a young boy already, he will show interest in the pregnancy only if the baby is a girl.

If a woman lies on her left when taking a rest, she's having a boy; if she lies on her right, she's having a girl.

Acne during pregnancy means a girl will be born.

Women often sleep with their pillow in a different place while pregnant: north for a boy, south for a girl.

Headaches during pregnancy mean a boy will be born.

Craving fruit during pregnancy means a girl is on the way.

If a woman suddenly feels her feet are colder, she will have a boy.

If a woman chooses the heel of a loaf of bread, the baby is a boy.

If the father-to-be stays slim during the pregnancy, the baby will be a girl.

A gray-haired maternal grandmother will have a grandson; a maternal grandmother with dyed hair or hair that is still its original color will have a granddaughter.

A woman with morning sickness early in pregnancy is expecting a girl.

When a needle on a thread held over a pregnant belly moves in circles, a boy is on the way.

Dull urine color indicates a girl; if it's neon yellow, the baby will be a boy.

If the mom-to-be craves sweets, a girl is on the way; salty cravings mean she's having a boy.

A pregnant woman whose nose spreads will have a boy.

A pregnant woman will pick up a key from the round end only if she's having a boy. If she picks it up at the long end, she's having a girl. If she grips it at the middle, twins are on the way.

◆

To improve her memory, ELEANOR ROOSEVELT ate three chocolate-covered garlic balls every day.

OXYDENTALLY ON PURPOSE

Some favorite oxymorons—the combination of two normally contradictory terms—old and new:

accurate estimate	easy labor
accurate rumors	elevated subway
act naturally	false hope
actual reenactment	fire water
alone together	firm estimate
altogether separate	freezer burn
amateur expert	good grief
among the first	ill health
authentic reproduction	jumbo shrimp
assistant supervisor	junk food
athletic scholarship	living dead
baby grand piano	midnight sun
bad health	minor disaster
bad sport	mud bath
balding hair	natural artifact
black light	new classic
books on tape	nothing much
brief survey	only choice
calm winds	open secret
certain risk	organized confusion
clearly confused	paid volunteer
clogged drain	peace force
cold sweat	plastic glasses
constant change	pretty ugly
constant variable	pure evil
deliberate mistake	quiet storm
detailed summary	recent history
devout atheist	recycling dump
double solitaire	rock opera

round corners	tentative conclusion
science fiction	thinking aloud
silent scream	tight slacks
steel wool	turned up missing
student teacher	virtual reality
sun shade	working vacation
taped live	

MIRANDA RIGHTS
Miranda v. Arizona, 384 U.S. 436 (1966)

Let's just say it's always good to know . . .

Before a law enforcement officer may question you regarding the possible commission of a crime, he or she must read you your Miranda rights. He or she must also make sure that you understand them.

WARNING OF RIGHTS

1. You have the right to remain silent and refuse to answer questions. Do you understand?
2. Anything you say can and will be used against you in a court of law. Do you understand?
3. You have the right to consult an attorney before speaking to the police and to have an attorney present during questioning now or in the future. Do you understand?
4. If you cannot afford an attorney, one will be appointed for you before any questioning if you wish. Do you understand?
5. If you decide to answer questions now without an attorney present you will still have the right to stop answering at any time until you talk to an attorney. Do you understand?
6. Knowing and understanding your rights as I have explained them to you, are you willing to answer my questions without an attorney present?

SLOT TALK
Slot Machine Terminology

Bonus feature: Some slot machines offer you a chance to win additional coins. This may be a second screen, free spin, and so on.

Coin size: The size of each bet

Coins per spin: The maximum number of coins that can be played for each spin

Payline: The combination of symbols that will result in the player getting paid off. In the old days, it was three cherries; many new machines offer several lines per play.

Payout percentages: What a slot machine pays out. For example, if a slot machine pays out 99 percent, that means that for every $100 that is taken in by the machine, $99 gets paid back out, meaning that the machine will "hold" $1 for $100. Payouts are listed, and a player should look for numbers in the high nineties.

Pay table: Winning combinations. You will find these listed on the slot machine or close by; the pay table explains how much each symbol on the machine pays out.

Progressive jackpot: A jackpot that continuously grows; that is, every time any player bets, a portion of that bet increments the jackpot; the higher the bet, the higher the increment.

Reels: This is the part of the machine where the symbols are displayed.

Wild symbol: Like a wild card, it's a symbol that counts as any other symbol, thus allowing a jackpot.

EXACTLY HOW SPECTACULAR?

New York City's famous Radio City Music Hall features its *Christmas Spectacular* for several weeks every holiday season. The renowned Radio City Rockettes are the primary stars of the show, but there are many other reasons this musical extravaganza is billed as "spectacular":

- There are more than thirteen hundred colorful costumes.
- The Rockettes change their costumes eight times during each show, often in as little as 78 seconds.
- The "Music Hall Menagerie" is a small herd of two donkeys, three camels, five sheep, and one horse.
- Radio City's Great Stage measures 144 feet by 66 feet. It is made up of three elevators, which may be set at any level from the sub-basement to 13 feet above the stage—a vertical drop of 40 feet. The orchestra uses a fourth elevator. Together, all four weigh 380,000 pounds.
- The "Mighty Wurlitzer Organ" is played during all performances: eleven rooms honeycomb around the theater housing the one-of-a-kind organ's 4,328 pipes and 1 million moving parts.
- Twenty-five hundred pounds of "snow" fall upon the Great Stage during the Christmas Spectacular's annual run.
- The complex sound system enables audiences to hear the orchestra from any seat in the theater—the traveling band car allows the orchestra to continue playing while moving back and forth on the stage and being raised and lowered on the elevators.

◆

The CRANBERRY, the blueberry, and the Concord blue grape are the only native fruits of North America.

WHAT FOOD GOES WITH TANG?

Astronautical meals do not require cooking as we know it here on Earth. The natural-state foods are in the same form as here on the ground; other foods are freeze-dried and vacuum-packed before takeoff and must be rehydrated with hot or cold water through the nozzle in the package.

ABBREVIATIONS:

RSB	Rehydratable spoon bowl (package shape)
RD	Rehydratable drink
IM	Intermediate moisture
D	Dehydrated
T	Thermostabilized
NS	Natural state

MENU ITEMS:

Bacon Squares (8) (IM)
Beef Jerky (IM)
Beef Stew (RSB)
Canadian Bacon and Applesauce (RSB)
Chicken Salad (8 ounces) (T)
Cinnamon Toasted Bread Cubes (4) (D)
Cocoa (RD)
Coffee (RD)
Cranberry-Orange Sauce (RSB)
Creamed Chicken Bites (6) (D)
Fruit Cocktail (RSB)
Grape Punch (RD)
Jellied Fruit Candy (IM)
Lobster Bisque (RSB)
Peach Ambrosia (RSB)
Peanut Cubes (4) (NS)

Pea Soup (RSB)
Pineapple Fruitcake (IM)
Pineapple-Grapefruit Drink (RD)
Pork and Scalloped Potatoes (RSB)
Scrambled Eggs (RSB)
Spiced Fruit Cereal (RSB)
Turkey Bites(4) (D)

◆

ARRGGGH! POISON!

Though sometimes useful in drug or food compositions, in their natural form these are absolute poison:

Aconite
Apple, Balsam
Apple, Bitter
Baneberry
Bloodroot
Bryony, Black
Bryony, European White
Bryony, White
Cabbage Tree
Calabar Bean
Calotropis
Cherry Laurel
Clematis
Coca, Bolivian
Cocculus, Indicus
Dropwort, Hemlock Water
Foxglove
Gelsemium

Hemlock
Hemlock, Water
Hemp, Indian
Ignatius Beans
Ivy, Poison
Laburnum
Laurel, Mountain
Lovage, Water
Mescal Buttons
Nightshade, Black
Nightshade, Deadly
Nux Vomica
Paris, Herb
Poppy, White
Saffron, Meadow
Spurges
Stavesacre
Strophanthus

PARTY PLANNING

Should you want to run for president—or perhaps just dog catcher—you can choose your affiliation from among these current United States minor political parties.

- Alaskan Independence Party
- Aloha Aina Party
- America First Party
- American Heritage Party
- American Independent Party
- American Nazi Party
- American Party
- American Reform Party
- Balanced Party
- Charter Party of Cincinnati, Ohio
- Christian Falangist Party of America
- Communist Party USA
- Conservative Party of New Jersey
- Conservative Party of New York State
- Constitutional Action Party
- Covenant Party (Northern Mariana Islands)
- Family Values Party
- Freedom Socialist Party
- Grassroots Party
- Independence Party of Minnesota
- Independent American Party
- Independent Citizens' Movement (US Virgin Islands)
- Labor Party
- Liberal Party (New York State)
- Liberty Union Party (Vermont)
- Light Party
- Marijuana Party

- Mountain Party (West Virginia)
- Natural Law Party
- New Party
- New Progressive Party of Puerto Rico
- New Union Party
- New York State Right to Life Party
- Peace and Freedom Party
- Personal Choice Party
- Popular Democratic Party of Puerto Rico
- Populist Party (unrelated to earlier so-named parties)
- Progressive Party (Vermont)
- Prohibition Party
- Puerto Rican Independence Party
- Reform Party
- Republican Moderate Party (Alaska)
- Revolutionary Communist Party
- Socialist Action
- Socialist Alternative
- Socialist Equality Party
- Socialist Labor Party
- Socialist Party USA
- Socialist Workers Party
- Southern Party
- Southern Independence Party
- Spartacist League
- The Greens/Green Party USA
- United Citizens Party
- U.S. Pacifist Party
- Vegetarian Party
- We the People Party
- Workers World Party
- Working Families Party
- Workers Party, USA

WATCH AND EARN

The top 100 movies in all-time worldwide box office, according to the International Movie Database (2005):

1. *Titanic* (1997)	$1,835,300,000
2. *The Lord of the Rings: The Return of the King* (2003)	1,129,219,252
3. *Harry Potter and the Sorcerer's Stone* (2001)	968,600,000
4. *Star Wars: Episode I, The Phantom Menace* (1999)	922,379,000
5. *The Lord of the Rings: The Two Towers* (2002)	921,600,000
6. *Jurassic Park* (1993)	919,700,000
7. *Shrek 2* (2004)	880,871,036
8. *Harry Potter and the Chamber of Secrets* (2002)	866,300,000
9. *Finding Nemo* (2003)	865,000,000
10. *The Lord of the Rings: The Fellowship of the Ring* (2001)	860,700,000
11. *Independence Day* (1996)	811,200,000
12. *Spider-Man* (2002)	806,700,000
13. *Star Wars* (1977)	797,900,000
14. *Star Wars: Episode III, Revenge of the Sith* (2005)	790,200,000
15. *Harry Potter and the Prisoner of Azkaban* (2004)	789,458,727
16. *Spider-Man 2* (2004)	783,577,893
17. *The Lion King* (1994)	783,400,000
18. *E.T. the Extra-Terrestrial* (1982)	756,700,000
19. *The Matrix Reloaded* (2003)	735,600,000

20.*Forrest Gump* (1994)	679,400,000
21.*The Sixth Sense* (1999)	661,500,000
22.*Pirates of the Caribbean: The Curse of the Black Pearl* (2003)	653,200,000
23.*Star Wars: Episode II, Attack of the Clones* (2002)	648,200,000
24.*The Incredibles* (2004)	624,037,578
25.*The Lost World: Jurassic Park* (1997)	614,300,000
26.*The Passion of the Christ* (2004)	604,370,943
27.*Men in Black* (1997)	587,200,000
28.*Star Wars: Episode VI, Return of the Jedi* (1983)	572,700,000
29.*Armageddon* (1998)	554,600,000
30.*Mission: Impossible II* (2000)	545,300,000
31.*Home Alone* (1990)	533,800,000
32.*Star Wars: Episode V, The Empire Strikes Back* (1980)	533,800,000
33.*Monsters, Inc.* (2001)	528,900,000
34.*The Day After Tomorrow* (2004)	527,939,919
35.*Ghost* (1990)	517,600,000
36.*Terminator 2: Judgment Day* (1991)	516,800,000
37.*Aladdin* (1992)	501,900,000
38.*War of the Worlds* (2005)	498,300,000
39.*Indiana Jones and the Last Crusade* (1989)	494,800,000
40.*Twister* (1996)	494,700,000
41.*Toy Story 2* (1999)	485,700,000
42.*Troy* (2004)	481,228,348
43.*Saving Private Ryan* (1998)	479,300,000
44.*Jaws* (1975)	470,600,000
45.*Pretty Woman* (1990)	463,400,000
46.*Bruce Almighty* (2003)	458,900,000
47.*The Matrix* (1999)	456,300,000

48. *Gladiator* (2000)	456,200,000
49. *Shrek* (2001)	455,100,000
50. *Mission: Impossible* (1996)	452,500,000
51. *Pearl Harbor* (2001)	450,400,000
52. *Ocean's Eleven* (2001)	444,200,000
53. *The Last Samurai* (2003)	435,400,000
54. *Tarzan* (1999)	435,200,000
55. *Meet the Fockers* (2004)	432,667,575
56. *Men in Black II* (2002)	425,600,000
57. *Die Another Day* (2002)	424,700,000
58. *Dances with Wolves* (1990)	424,200,000
59. *Cast Away* (2000)	424,000,000
60. *The Matrix Revolutions* (2003)	424,000,000
61. *Mrs. Doubtfire* (1993)	423,200,000
62. *The Mummy Returns* (2001)	418,700,000
63. *Terminator 3: Rise of the Machines* (2003)	418,200,000
64. *The Mummy* (1999)	413,300,000
65. *Batman* (1989)	413,200,000
66. *Rain Man* (1988)	412,800,000
67. *The Bodyguard* (1992)	410,900,000
68. *Signs* (2002)	407,900,000
69. *X2* (2003)	406,400,000
70. *Robin Hood: Prince of Thieves* (1991)	390,500,000
71. *Gone with the Wind* (1939)	390,500,000
72. *Raiders of the Lost Ark* (1981)	383,900,000
73. *Grease* (1978)	379,800,000
74. *Beauty and the Beast* (1991)	378,300,000
75. *Ice Age* (2002)	378,300,000
76. *Godzilla* (1998)	375,800,000
77. *What Women Want* (2000)	370,800,000
78. *The Fugitive* (1993)	368,700,000
79. *Hitch* (2005)	367,600,000
80. *True Lies* (1994)	365,200,000

81.*Die Hard: With a Vengeance* (1995)	365,000,000
82.*Notting Hill* (1999)	363,000,000
83.*Jurassic Park III* (2001)	362,900,000
84.*There's Something About Mary* (1998)	360,000,000
85.*Planet of the Apes* (2001)	358,900,000
86.*The Flintstones* (1994)	358,500,000
87.*Toy Story* (1995)	358,100,000
88.*Minority Report* (2002)	358,000,000
89.*A Bug's Life* (1998)	357,900,000
90.*The Exorcist* (1973)	357,500,000
91.*My Big Fat Greek Wedding* (2002)	356,500,000
92.*Basic Instinct* (1992)	352,700,000
93.*The World Is Not Enough* (1999)	352,000,000
94.*Madagascar* (2005)	351,800,000
95.*Golden Eye* (1995)	351,500,000
96.*Ocean's Twelve* (2004)	351,331,634
97.*Back to the Future* (1985)	350,600,000
98.*Se7en* (1995)	350,100,000
99.*Who Framed Roger Rabbit* (1988)	349,200,000
100. *Hannibal* (2001)	349,200,000

RELIGION AND SPORTS—TOGETHER AT LAST!

The House of David was a barnstorming baseball team from Benton Harbor, Michigan. The House of David Players were all white, but they frequently traveled with and played exhibition games against the top teams in the Negro Leagues.

The House of David was a religious community whose founder was a sports enthusiast. The community also had a girls' baseball team.

TEN-HUT!
Military Ranks

NAVY	ARMY
Fleet admiral (wartime use only)	General of the army
Admiral	General
Vice admiral	Lieutenant general
Rear admiral (upper half)	Major general
Rear admiral (lower half)	Brigadier general
Captain	Colonel
Commander	Lieutenant colonel
Lieutenant commander	Major
Lieutenant	Captain
Lieutenant junior grade	First lieutenant
Ensign	Second lieutenant
Master chief petty officer of the navy	Sergeant major of the army
Master chief petty officer	Command sergeant major
Senior chief petty officer	Sergeant major
Chief petty officer	First sergeant
Petty officer first class	Master sergeant
Petty officer second class	Sergeant first class
Petty officer third class	Staff sergeant
Seaman	Sergeant
Seaman apprentice	Corporal
Seaman recruit	Specialist
	Private first class
	Private

MARINE CORPS

General
Lieutenant general
Major general
Brigadier general
Colonel
Lieutenant colonel
Major
Captain
First lieutenant
Second lieutenant
Sergeant Major or Master
   gunnery sergeant
Master Sergeant or First
   Sergeant
Gunnery sergeant
Staff sergeant
Sergeant
Corporal
Lance corporal
Private first class
Private
Cadet
Recruit

AIR FORCE

General
Lieutenant general
Major general
Brigadier general
Colonel
Lieutenant colonel
Major
Captain
First Lieutenant
Second lieutenant
Command chief master
   sergeant
Senior master sergeant
Master sergeant
Technical sergeant
Staff sergeant
Senior airman
Airman first class
Airman
Airman basic
Cadet
Recruit

SO BAD THEY'RE GOOD

There are many common drugs made from poisonous plants.
Here are some of the most familiar:

Plant	Drug	Use
Amazonian liana	Curare	Muscle relaxant
Annual mugwort	Artemisinin	Antimalarial
Autumn crocus	Colchichine	Antihumor agent
Coca	Cocaine	Local anaesthetic
Common thyme	Thymol	Antifungal
Deadly nightshade (belladonna)	Atropine	Anticholinergic
Dog button (nux-vomica)	Strychnine	Central nervous stimulant
Ergot fungus	Ergotamine	Analgesic
Foxglove	Digitoxin, digitalis	Cardiotonic
Indian snakeroot	Resperine	Antihypertensive
Meadowsweet	Salicylate	Analgesic
Mexican yam	Diosgenin	Birth control pill
Opium poppy	Codeine, morphine	Analgesic
Pacific yew	Toxol	Antihumor agent
Rosy periwinkle	Vincristine, vinblastine	Antileukemia
Thornapple	Scopolamine	Sedative
Velvet bean	L-dopa	Antiparkinsonian
White willow	Salicylic acid	Topical analgesic
Yellow cinchona	Quinine	Antimalaria, antipyretic